ZOMBIE LOYALISTS

Peter Shankman is the author of *Nice Companies Finish First: Why Cutthroat Management Is Over—and Collaboration Is In; Customer Service: New Rules for a Social-Enabled World;* and *Can We Do That?! Outrageous PR Stunts That Work—and Why Your Company Needs Them.*

ZOMBIE LOYALISTS

USING GREAT SERVICE TO CREATE RABID FANS

PETER SHANKMAN

palgrave
macmillan

ZOMBIE LOYALISTS
Copyright © Peter Shankman, 2015.

First published in 2015 by PALGRAVE MACMILLAN® TRADE
in the United States—a division of St. Martin's Press LLC, 175 Fifth
Avenue, New York, NY 10010.

Palgrave® and Macmillan® are registered trademarks in the United
States, the United Kingdom, Europe and other countries.

ISBN 978-1-137-27966-8

Library of Congress Cataloging-in-Publication Data

Shankman, Peter.
    Zombie loyalists : using great service to create rabid fans / Peter
Shankman.
    pages   cm
    ISBN 978-1-137-27966-8 (alk. paper)
    1. Customer services. 2. Customer relations. 3. Customer loyalty.
I. Title.
HF5415.5.S51943   2014
658.8'12—dc23

                                                            2014024995

A catalogue record of the book is available from the British Library.

Design by Letra Libre, Inc.

First edition: January 2015

10 9 8 7 6 5 4 3 2

Printed in the United States of America.

CONTENTS

ACKNOWLEDGMENTS

This book wouldn't exist without the help of countless people, a few of whom I'm privileged to name here.

Emily Carleton is every writer's dream, as she's hands down the best editor in the known universe. With her on this journey was everyone from Palgrave, as well as Carol Mann and her awesome book agency. Glad to be one of your clients, Carol!

On the personal side, Meagan Walker is the most patient and loyal assistant anyone could ever have, and I'm fortunate that she's mine. David Roher, Ty Francis, and Todd Evans listened to me complain from start to finish, and I'm grateful for all three of you. Ryan Shell also listened to me complain, usually on a bike-training ride through Central Park at 5 a.m. For that, and for making me faster, I'm super appreciative. Steven Costello showed me what it means to be amazing to the people you have to get the people you want, and I'm fortunate to call him and everyone at Steiner Sports a friend.

And lastly, this book couldn't have been remotely dreamed of without my thousands upon thousands of Facebook friends, followers, and subscribers. I'm so fortunate that you allow me into your lives on a daily basis, and I never, ever take you for granted.

I always say family first! With that, thank you, as always, Mom, Dad, Alan, Amy, Carol, Fern, Hillary, Stacy, Seporah, Todd, and the rest of my family, always there with a smile when I needed it.

Lastly, in the end, I will always be a Zombie Loyalist to two people: my wife Kira and my beautiful daughter Jessa. I'm the luckiest guy in the world because I have you both.

1

THE WALKING DEAD?

PLEASE. LET'S TALK ABOUT *REAL* ZOMBIES

Not now, Haley! I'm zombie dancing with my son!

—Stan Smith, *American Dad*

Right now, there are two reasons you've picked up this book (or are currently reading the first five pages on Amazon).

1. You mistakenly thought this was a cool new science-fiction novel about zombies.
2. You know that there is nothing better to bring in new customers than current customers. Not advertising, not marketing, not social media, and not public relations (PR)— *nothing* in the world brings in more new customers than happy current customers.

If your reason is 1, then I'm sorry, you've been misled. I do recommend David Wellington, however, as his book *Monster Island* is spectacular.

But . . . if your choice is 2, well then, my friend, welcome to the fray. My name is Peter Shankman, and I'm going to help you build your army. You're going to learn how to build an army of customers so strong, so stuck on you, so in love with your business, so downright loyal, they're going to take over your advertising, marketing, and PR, and they're going to do it better than you ever could yourself. You're going to build an army for your business the likes of which you've never seen—the likes of which you can't even begin to imagine.

Remember the guys from *300*? The really muscular ones with the painted-on abs? They wouldn't last five seconds against the Zombie Loyalists you're going to create.

This army is going to virtually *print* you money. It's going to do it for you every day. It's going to make your business one of the most important things in their lives. In some cases, *the* most important thing. And that'll get a bit creepy. But it's going to be okay.

You're going to learn how to take care of your army. How to train it. How to feed and water it. How to make it happy. How to nurture it. You'll learn how to command its attention at any moment. You'll learn how the loyalty of your zombies is directly proportional to your loyalty to them. You're going to be amazed, astounded, left wondering, "Can it really be that simple?" But once you get started, you'll realize, "Holy crap, it really is."

We're going to build you an army of Zombie Loyalists, and it's going to take over the world for you. Well, maybe not the world. But it'll at least bring you some great new customers and a bunch of new revenue. (But hey, maybe the world. You never know.)

But I'm getting ahead of myself. Let's talk a little background first.

When I told my best friend that my next book was going to be about customer service and zombies, his reaction was what you'd expect from any normal person.

"Zombies. Seriously? You're writing a business book about game-changing customer service, and the theme is zombies? And your publisher agreed to this?"

My friend had known me for *eight years;* you'd think he'd have been a bit more prepared for the way my brain functions.

Anyhow, who am I, and why are you listening to me?

Well, as I said, my name is Peter Shankman. I'm many things. I'm an entrepreneur who has successfully sold three companies. I'm an investor or advisor to at least a dozen companies, including pure tech start-ups, clothing companies, a company that makes lip balm for the teen and tween markets, and even NASA. (Yes, NASA has a civilian advisory council, and I'm honored to serve on it.) My last book, *Nice Companies Finish First,* explains why companies that put "nice" over "cutthroat" tend to make a lot more money.

I keep a blog at www.shankman.com; run Mastermind conferences all over the world at www.shankminds.com; and cohost *The Mistake Podcast,* a podcast on making mistakes, at www.themistakepodcast.com. Those three things keep me traveling about 300,000 miles per year, and that traveling gives me tons of time to observe and write about what I observe. In fact, the ideas for all three of my previous books came to me on flights, and this one is no exception. Here's what happened.

I was flying home from a business meeting in Los Angeles and had just boarded my United flight. As I was getting settled, I removed my MacBook Air, iPad, power cord, and headphones from my jacket. Yes, you read that right, *from my jacket.* I'm on the advisory board of a company called SCOTTeVEST—a clothing company that makes travel clothing, including jackets with tons of pockets, like the one I wear whenever I fly.

The person next to me couldn't take her eyes off my jacket as I removed more and more things, like 26 clowns getting out of a Volkswagen. When I sat down, she immediately asked me about the jacket, and I gushed over how many pockets it had, how I was able to do four days in Tokyo with nothing but the jacket, and so on. For the sake of full disclosure, I mentioned to her I was on the company's board as well.

"I would hope so" was her reply. "You've completely sold me on it. Between watching you pull all your stuff out and how you talked to me about it, I'm going online right now and ordering one!"

"Oh, well, here—please use this code," I said, and gave her a code for 20 percent off the cost of anything on the site. Floored, she proceeded to order one for herself, one for her husband, one for each of her three kids, and one for her assistant.

She probably spent $650 to $750 dollars in under five minutes. Now here's where it gets really interesting. About halfway through the flight, she leaned over and showed me a page in the *SkyMall* catalog. You know, the catalog in the seat-back pocket of every single airplane that sells things like automatic cat groomers and tequila holders that will get your drink down to a temperature of absolute zero.

"This is the jacket I just bought, right?" she said, pointing to the SeV ad in *SkyMall*.

"Yup," I replied. "That's them."

"Gotta tell you," she said, "you make a much more convincing advertisement than the one in this magazine."

That's when it hit me. This woman just bought five jackets not because she saw an ad and not because I was "selling" her on it. She bought the jackets based on *my* enthusiasm for them. She bought the jackets because I couldn't stop explaining how amazing they are.

I was the best advertisement she'd ever seen, and the excitement in my eyes over being able to keep my 15-inch laptop in my jacket was enough to send her over the edge. When I showed her the two secret money compartments built into the inside of the coat as well as the space for my toothbrush(!), she was sold.

At that moment, on that airplane, I was a Zombie Loyalist for SCOTTeVEST, and I still am to this day. I'd done what all zombies are trained to do—I converted a regular person into one of the flock. How many jackets do you think *her* recommendations to *her* network are going to sell?

I created a Zombie Loyalist in seat 2-B. And it was good.

WHAT ZOMBIES CAN TEACH YOU
ABOUT YOUR BUSINESS

I consult with companies all around the globe about how to fix their customer service, which, unsurprisingly, usually sucks. The problem is, most CEOs think they're doing just fine when it comes to customer service.

Prepare yourself for some frightening numbers:

- 80 percent of businesses believe they deliver "superior" customer service.

• Only 8 percent of those businesses' customers agree.

Holy disconnect, Batman!! Think about that for a second—you've got CEOs in their ivory towers, all happy and content because they're being fed BS from all their yes-men. Then, on the customer service floor, you have all the frontline responders, apologizing for the mistakes the company is causing but unable to actually do anything about them because they're not empowered. And why aren't they? Because their bosses aren't empowered to empower them. Follow it all the way up the chain, and you get a CEO who doesn't see a need to change anything because "everything's fine."

This is a huge, huge problem, and it affects almost every company to some extent.

Unfortunately, this blindness is nothing new. We see it all the time—just look at your Facebook feed. No, really. Go look at your Facebook feed. Right now. I'll wait.

How many scrolls did you have to go through before you found the first customer service complaint? They're all there. And that's what makes today's customer service mentality so damn annoying. It's obvious to everyone in the company that there are problems, except to the people who can actually fix them. And that just *so* needs to change.

A few months ago, my company commissioned an infographic to show to potential clients who feel that they need help improving their customer service. What we learned from this infographic was so startling that I'll revisit it throughout the course of this book just to drive the point home.

Imagine that you plucked an employee from today, say, a gas station attendant, and sent them back in time to work in the same job in 1955. How long do you think he'd last in 1955?

A few hours, at most. He'd have no concept of what it meant to be in a pressed uniform, run to a car when it pulled up, or check the oil while the gas was pumping while also cleaning the windshield wipers and checking the tire pressure.

He wouldn't know because he'd be used to sitting behind his bulletproof partition, paying attention to a customer only when making change or handing out a bathroom key.

As a result of such changes, customers today *expect* to be treated like crap, and a fair number of customer service employees have problems providing even the minimum their title promises.

The problem is, if crap service is considered the norm, there's no wiggle room when an employee has a bad day and really goes off on a customer. If all we can expect on the best day is grunts and the occasional mumbled "thanks," then the smallest slip can lose a customer for life. And that's where our first stat comes in:

In 2012, 77 percent of customers in the United States reported at least one experience of rudeness in an interaction with a customer service representative.

That's a huge number. It means that more than three-quarters of your customers had at least one experience with a rude customer service person—a waiter, a mechanic, a phone rep, a sales clerk, a flight attendant, an usher, you name it. Over 75 percent of your customers had a bad experience at least once in a 365-day period.

When you stop and think about it, it's pretty amazing. As I said, given our abysmal expectations, an employee *really* needs to go out of his or her way to be rude enough for a customer to notice and report it.

PREEMPTIVE STRIKES: WHY YOUR EMPLOYEES SHOULD BE YOUR FIRST "VICTIMS"

Rudeness happens for countless reasons. As a friend of mine who runs customer relations for a major hotel chain once told me, "Peter, we simply can't assume that every employee is going to be able to be Mary Freaking Sunshine every single day, it's not humanly possible."

I get that, and I agree wholeheartedly. Employees have bad days, just like customers do. But if you're in charge of customer service, you can do tremendous things, at little cost, to prevent those employee moods from affecting the customer.

First off, you can implement preemptive strikes that keep your employees happier than the average employee at the average company, then they'll treat your customers better than customers at the average company, so when the employee *does* have a bad day, the effect will be lessened and the impact and aftershocks will be much less dangerous. You might even be able to prevent the employee's bad day long before he or she ever interacts with the customer.

The value of any employee is quite measurable—it obviously costs a heck of a lot less to keep the employees you have than it does to hire and train new ones. It's not rocket science to understand that those employees who feel valued provide better quality service to their customers.

So how do you get employees to feel like they matter? How do you show employees that they're important to the company as a whole, not just another cog in the wheel?

It's never what you think it is.

Several months ago, my customer service consultancy was brought in to work on a massive customer service overhaul for a major consumer transportation hub. We spent weeks interviewing hundreds of employees at this hub, and we were shocked to find that time and time again, the employees told us that what they wanted most was to feel like they had a voice in the company—that the company noticed their actions, appreciated what they did, and valued them as people.

They told us over and over that this was even more important to them than monetary rewards. We were floored.

Turns out they weren't the exception: Consultancy company The Geek Factory, Inc. conducted anonymous interviews with employees at a major Fortune 50 company. Almost 60 percent of these employees said that they would be more inclined to work harder, take better care of their customers, and be more "present" in the workplace if they simply felt like their employer cared about them. In other words, they felt like they didn't matter. How can you possibly motivate employees to care about customers when employees themselves feel like they don't matter?

When human resource professionals conduct exit interviews with customer service employees, "not being listened to" is always up there as one of the reasons for leaving.

Not listening to employees is a tradition dating back hundreds of years, almost always with negative results. Look at the rail lines that were laid in Europe—hundreds, if not thousands of workers died from unsafe conditions, despite their countless attempts to tell management what was happening. The end result was strikes, fights, work stoppages, and uprisings across Europe until workers' demands were met.

In America, the formation of unions was a direct result of companies not listening to their employees, until the companies found themselves without a choice.

Every work stoppage, labor action, or shutdown in any company, big or small, can be directly traced back to employees feeling like they don't have a voice or that their voice wasn't heard.

Heck, failing to listen to employees has even cost lives, as when Morton-Thiokol chose not to pay attention to engineer Roger Boisjoly, who warned that the O-rings designed for Space Shuttle Challenger wouldn't hold up in colder weather. We all know what happened there.

It's very simple, really: Employees need to know that, all the way up the chain, people will listen. From managers to directors, from vice presidents to the CEO, a company's corporate culture has to involve listening to its employees and valuing their contributions to the company. If employees don't feel valued, why should they bother making sure customers do?

You're going to learn how to treat your employees like superheroes. Superhero employees can create Zombie Loyalist customers every single time they interact with them.

WHY ZOMBIES?

Now then: Let's shift from employees for a second, and let me tell you about zombies.

While I'm sure you've heard of a zombie before (undead, eats people's brains, infecting them and turning them into zombies, re- peat cycle), chances are high that you've never met an actual zom- bie up close. I say this based on logic. If you have, then it's more than likely that they've infected you, and you're a zombie too. If that's the case, then reading this book isn't high on your list of priorities.

So I'm going to assume you've never met a zombie. That's fine. Here's all you need to know about them:

Overall, they're not the nicest of people. They rarely say "excuse me" after bumping into you, and the chances of one of them holding the door open for you as you're coming in out of the rain is slim, at best.

There are two reasons that zombies don't have the most basic etiquette that society expects:

1. Zombies are designed almost exclusively to feed, enabling them to produce more zombies.
2. Zombies don't care about *anything else in the world* but reason 1.

When humans are bitten by a zombie and become zombies them- selves, everything they've ever learned in their entire lives—every rule of law, every how-to-act lesson, every modicum of common sense they have goes right out the window. When humans become zombies, only one thing matters: "How will I get my next feeding?" It doesn't matter if you're the President of the United States or a jani- tor at an elementary school: To a zombie, you're just meat. If you're not meat, you don't matter.

That's some pretty hard-core internal wiring, huh? Imagine not caring about *anything else!* Imaging not caring about love, or the rules of polite society, or whether the Mets won, even though they probably didn't. Imagine not caring about your job, or what number you are in line at the deli. Seems crazy, huh? But zombies don't have the ability to reason or higher-level cognition. Zombies simply know that to survive, they need to feed. So they feed, and everything else be damned.

Now here's a thought: What if you could take that same singular zombie focus and impart it to your customers? Imagine what would happen if you could turn each customer into a zombie? (Not real zombies, of course, because, well, you'd be primarily responsible for the extinction of humankind.) But what if your customers lived not just for feeding *but just for patronizing your business?*

Imagine if you could make your customers so in love with you, so amazed at their experience with you, each and every time, that they'd have no *choice* but to tell the world how great you are? They couldn't even conceive of going to your competitor, because they're so programmed to shop with you. They don't just come back; they bring friends. Lots of friends. And they do this . . . Every. Single. Time. Remember, we know this about zombies: They feed in packs. Once you're a zombie, you rarely do anything alone.

While you probably haven't met an actual zombie up close, you've no doubt met Zombie Loyalists. You probably interact with them every day—they're your friends, your relatives, your coworkers, you name it.

They're people so passionate about something they love that they'll tell you about it at every opportunity. Think of the guy who you work with who *always* wants to go to lunch at the Olive Garden: "I just love their breadsticks! They're amazing! Let's go to the Olive Garden for lunch today."

Or it's the frequent flier who goes out of his way to fly one specific airline, going so far as to get up early, come back late, and make three separate connecting flights when another airline has a middle-of-the-day nonstop to the same location. He's a Zombie Loyalist.

It could even be your wife—mine is a Zombie Loyalist for Starbucks. If it's not a Venti Soy Latte, Extra Hot, from Starbucks, she won't drink it. (The funny thing about this is that I'm a Zombie Loyalist for Dunkin' Donuts. So, that causes some grief in our marriage.)

Now imagine an army of Zombie Loyalists, waiting to do your bidding. All you have to do is create a culture that empowers your employees to infect your customers with amazing service. One little bite is all it takes to build your army of Zombie Loyalists and set them loose on an unsuspecting world, causing a pandemic of loyalty you have to see to believe!

I've been building armies of Zombie Loyalists for some of the biggest companies in the world, and I've had a blast doing it. I've helped companies massively increase their customer base, brand awareness, and, most important, bottom-line revenue. I build Zombie Loyalist armies for businesses for one simple reason: No one believes how amazing your business is *if you're the one who has to tell them.* But if you can get your customers to tell their friends how awesome you are, if you can turn your current customers into Zombie Loyalists who infect everyone they meet, then you have something real. You have a Zombie Loyalist army that will do whatever you ask, buy every product you sell, and go out of its way to buy from you and no one else, no matter how inconvenient it might be. And what you're holding right now is the field training guide.

REAL-WORLD ZOMBIES

Now I want you to think back to that last time you had a truly amazing experience as a customer. Perhaps it was on a plane. Maybe you got through the nightmare that is TSA in under three minutes, and when you got to your gate, you found that your initial seat, which was something horrible like 34-Bathroom, had been magically upgraded by a nice gate agent to 2-D. All of a sudden, you went from the back of the bus to the front!

You don't realize it at the time, but you're in the first stages of zombie transformation. The upgrade was the first bite, and you probably didn't even notice. (Most of the newly infected don't.) But a germ was just implanted in your brain. Call it a "loyalty embryo." This embryo was just absorbed by your body, and it's planting roots in your customer consciousness in real time.

But, as I said, you didn't notice it at all. All you notice, as you sit down in your new (much wider) seat, is the flight attendant coming over and handing you a pre-takeoff drink. Then your jaw drops as she addresses you by name and hangs up your jacket.

See, creating Zombie Loyalists is actually incredibly easy—much easier than, say, catching the common cold. Why? Because our brains and minds are already riddled with the primer that allows Zombie Loyalty to thrive: It's called "service crapitis," and it's a horrible disease, fatal to companies and brands, big and small, all around the world. Once one company infects a customer with service crapitis, that customer is then the perfect target to become a Zombie Loyalist to a *different company*.

Think about it: We expect our fast food order to be screwed up. We expect to go to the dry cleaners on Thursday, when we were told our clothing would be ready, only to be told it won't be ready until Monday. We expect the car dealership to overcharge us, and we expect the airplane to be delayed.

In other words, we ingest a constant stream of service crapitis every day, so much that our defenses against becoming a Zombie Loyalist to a brand that's even 1 percent better than crap are weak or nonexistent. It takes very little to turn a dissatisfied customer into a Zombie Loyalist.

Tip: No one wakes up expecting to become a Zombie Loyalist, and that works in your favor.

If that one-level-above-crap treatment continues, the infection gets stronger, and our brains start to mutate from "dissatisfied customer," to "impressed customer," to "I can't believe how amazing this company is," and then, finally, to Zombie Loyalist. Once customers have reached the Zombie Loyalist stage, there's virtually no way that any other brand or company can save them. They're loyal to the company that first made them zombies, and all they want to do is tell the world about them.

WHAT GREAT SERVICE LOOKS LIKE

Think about your favorite store for a second. The place where you always shop, the place to which you'll drive an extra 15 minutes because they know you, the service is amazing, and the experience is never anything short of magical.

Did you ever stop and think about the fact that you're going *out of your way* to give this company more money? In fact, you're spending extra time and money to make sure that your business is given to this company. In this hyper–convenience-conscious world, that's pretty huge, huh?

Let's take it a step further: What if you were *such* a fan of your favorite company that you'd welcome the opportunity to simply learn more about it? Perhaps in a behind-the-scenes type of way, offered only to a lucky, select few? Throughout the course of this book, we'll talk many times about how experience is the most valuable prize to a Zombie Loyalist, and you'll learn how to create amazing experiences to help grow your Zombie Loyalist army.

With that said, can you imagine being *so* loyal to a company that if it asked you to spend a weekend day working for it, you'd consider it a gift? Well, that's exactly what United Airlines asked me and 19 other Zombie Loyalists to do one Saturday last year. And we all did it—without a second's hesitation.

Or, as my wife said as I was leaving the house that morning, "So the company you give tons of money to each year is asking you to spend your day off *working* for them, for free, and you're doing it, *and* you're happy about it?"

Of course I was. Who else in my world would ever get a chance to load and unload baggage, push a plane off the gate, or board passengers? And therein lies the secret: A company that I already love was letting me learn more about it, in a way that very few people got to experience, and I got to share that with the world. In essence, I got to say, "Look what I'm doing that you're not." *I got to brag.* And it was an amazing experience. I documented the heck out of it on Facebook, my blog, Instagram, Twitter, you name it. Why? Because I could, and you couldn't. Like I said, I got to brag. And no matter how humble we all are, human beings will always take a certain satisfaction in being able to enjoy something others can't.

As we'll discuss, the new social economy that we're all a part of runs on two things: bragging and drama. Either of those things can create Zombie Loyalists, for your company or for someone else's. If the world is truly going to end one day at the hands of a zombie apocalypse, wouldn't you want those zombies to be loyal to you?

I fly a lot, and so do hundreds of my friends. While most people see air travel as an inconvenience to be dealt with, a few of us look at it with excitement almost every time. Why? Because United goes out of its way to make our experience great because we're loyal fliers. Now, United strives to make each flight a great one for every passenger, but it extends extra perks to those who fly all the time. It continues to work to earn our continued loyalty, and it becomes a

The author showing his Zombie Loyalty to his favorite airline—and probably delaying 250 passengers in the process.

win for both entities—for me, the Zombie Loyalist, and for United, which gets not only *my* revenue but the revenue of all the zombies I've bitten. In other words, when I fly with other people, I make sure they fly United as well.

In the last example, United is not only working to keep me as one of its Zombie Loyalists, but it's also working to prevent any other company from curing me. When you break it down, those two things have to be symbiotic.

Albert Einstein once said, "You can't simultaneously prevent and prepare for war." The opposite logic applies here—you have to care for your zombies while also constantly reinfecting them so they'll never leave.

Fact: Zombie Loyalists that you've worked so hard to infect can be cured only by a combination of two antidotes given at the same time:

1. Crap service from you.
2. Awesome service from your competitor.

To put it another way, you constantly need to be stepping up your game, or you'll lose your loyalists, and, worse, they'll become zombies for another brand, most likely your biggest competitor. And there's nothing worse than losing a zombie. Lose one zombie, and it's a slippery slope to losing them all. While it's hard to lose a zombie, it does happen—and you need to make sure you're constantly working to ensure it doesn't happen.

There is hope, though. While zombies can be cured by your competitors, it's not an overnight process. Certain steps have to be taken, in a very specific sequence, to cause you to lose a Zombie Loyalist to your competitor. Later in the book, we'll discuss ways to prevent this and ways to make sure that you're not leaving your customers ripe for infection by your competitors.

In chapter 2, you're going to shake up your entire business from top to bottom. See, the majority of companies don't breed Zombie

Loyalists because their breeding ground (employees and management) don't understand why it's necessary to do so. So we're going to examine your company, identify your top barriers to creating Zombie Loyalists, and eliminate them. In chapter 3, you're going to learn how to create a breeding ground. To create Zombie Loyalists, all the pieces have to be in place, and it starts with your employees. It simply doesn't work any other way. Imagine going to a restaurant to find one waiter who simply rocks. He knows you, knows what you like, has your favorite drink prepared as he sees you walking in the door. You'd be fond of him, without question. *But* . . . if he's the only zombie maker in the establishment, you probably won't love him enough to return over and over again. While he might be trying his hardest to make you a Zombie Loyalist, if the host doesn't seat you in a timely manner, if the food the waiter delivers tastes terrible, and if the place is dirty, you won't go back, no matter how amazing your awesome waiter is. In the end, it has to be a unilateral effort from your entire company, from the CEO down to the person who cleans the tables. There needs to be a *company culture* designed to create Zombie Loyalists. We'll look at some of the companies that have woven this culture into the fabric of everything they do and show you exactly what it takes to make every one of your employees *want* to create Zombie Loyalists.

By the end of chapter 3, you're going to be talking about zombies to your coworkers, and they're going to look at you very strangely. I'm just warning you of that now. It will happen.

As we begin chapter 4, we're going to talk about infecting that first customer. Maybe you're a start-up that's just launched, or maybe you're taking over a business from former management who simply didn't get it, or perhaps you've finally convinced the C-suite that it needs to change. Whatever the reason, one thing has to happen before anything else can:

You have to infect someone. You have to create that first zombie. Until you do that, the loyalists won't come, the army won't amass, and the slaying of your competitors won't begin. You need to create that first infection.

Remember that movie—I think it was *Interview with a Vampire*, where Brad Pitt's character, after realizing he'd been bitten, knew he had to drink blood to survive, but couldn't bring himself to do it? He was close to death, all he had to do was drink blood, but he just couldn't, because, let's face it, drinking blood is kinda gross, until finally, he realized he was going to die if he didn't. So he did, and it tasted *good*. He felt life rushing back into his body, and from that moment on, he was totally cool with the whole blood-drinking thing. That's exactly what happens before, during, and after you infect your first zombie.

It's hard to force a company to change. There's no doubt about that, and you'll never get any arguments from me about it. Believe me—I've worked with Fortune 100 companies all the way down to mom-and-pop stores. Getting an entire company to change for the better is as hard as the vampire biting into that first neck. But once it happens, once the culture is established and *the results prove out*, once you've made all the conditions in your company petri-dish optimal for Zombie Loyalist creation, no one in your company will want to go back to the old way of doing things. Because hey, there's no business like a business that creates Zombie Loyalists.

Chapter 5 gets into the meat of the book—building an army.

It's not enough to have one or two Zombie Loyalists. To build your army, you need to make *every one of your customers* realize that they want—nay, *need*—to fight for you. They *need* to infect others for you. Your zombies have to have their eyes and ears open, scanning for any trouble that might be coming down the road for your business. They have to be ready to defend, attack, and create more zombies for your business on a moment's notice. They need to truly believe there's nothing they won't do for your business, because they love only you. Remember: You turned them into zombies. Treat them well, and they'll never leave your side.

But—notice I said "Treat them well." Throughout chapter 5, you'll learn tips and tricks to keep your zombies loyal and, more important, how to get them to infect others for you. Remember: You can't build your army simply by telling people how great you are.

You need to show them, and then let those people go out and infect others for you.

Or, to quote the line I end almost every corporate keynote with: "You get the customers you *want* by being beyond awesome to the customers you *have*."

Imagine having an army with no means of transport. Well, it would be great at defending one place but probably not so good at conquering and pillaging, huh? I doubt Genghis Khan would have been as good at taking over whole civilizations if he had to do it all from his living room. No, he had to be mobile.

The same rules apply to your zombie army, and in chapter 6, you'll learn how to get your zombies to infect others. Essentially, how to share. Having a great army of Zombie Loyalists won't do anything for you if they don't have a way to infect others. And while actual zombies do it by walking slowly with their arms outstretched and biting anyone they encounter, Zombie Loyalists do it by talking— whether in person or online, using all the various social tools at their disposal. And believe me, they talk. We all know that guy who's crazy about that one company and is constantly recommending it to you. That's a Zombie Loyalist, and that's who you want to create. To do that, though, you have to provide people with the right things to say, show, post, tweet, share, and so on. This could be everything from photo opportunities to responding to their tweets, from special deliveries to unexpected upgrades. . . . You've got to give your zombies content, content, and more content. You've got to give them reasons to post, reasons to share, and reasons to infect other zombies. Let's face it: A Zombie Loyalist's preferred (some might say only) method of infection is sharing. Your job is to make sure they're sharing what you want them to share so that they infect others and create more Zombie Loyalists for your business. I'll give you a bunch of examples of how companies big and small are doing just this.

Now we come to chapter 7, the chapter that should scare you the most: "You Lost a Zombie!" There are few things that can destroy your business to the core faster than losing a zombie. One customer who has fully recovered from being your zombie can do two very bad things to your business:

1. He's ripe for infection from your competitor (and believe me, your competitors know all about your best zombies).
2. If he's infected by your competitor, the chances are very good that he's going to immediately try and take his whole army with him. Every one of your customers previously infected by him are now at risk for a full recovery and reinfection by your competitor.

In other words, one lost Zombie Loyalist can take hundreds of other Zombie Loyalists with him or her, and in the blink of an eye, you could be in a serious world of hurt.

You've got to act fast to get this customer back and reinfected. It doesn't matter what you did to lose the person; what matters is what you do to get him or her back. Depending on how much of a Zombie Loyalist this customer was, this could be anything from a public apology all the way to a beer with the CEO. Whatever you do, you need to do it quick, do it right, and make sure you get in front of the problem, solve it, and keep your zombie. This is the moment where every single one of your competitors is watching, ready to pounce and try to steal your zombie. And if you don't act fast, that's exactly what's going to happen. Remember: A former zombie makes the worst kind of hater. Say I used to love your brand, but then you went south, and now I hate your brand. Well, I'm going to take all my loyalty somewhere else and probably talk about everything you did wrong and everything you could have done right to save me but didn't. Why? Because I'm now a scorned Zombie Loyalist. And in the eyes of your business, that's the worst thing I could ever be.

You know the phrase "Haters gonna hate"? Well, I've got a new one for you: Zombies gonna zom. Because, at the end of the day, if, over time, I came to feel "special" whenever I interacted with your company and now I no longer do, I'm going to want to feel special again. And if you're not making me feel special? If you're not working to make me a Zombie Loyalist anymore? I'll simply go find a company that will. And I'll love it big time. Why? Because, my friends, zombies gonna zom. So, in chapter 8, you're going to learn how to get that zombie back.

Strangely enough, it's harder to get back one Zombie Loyalist than it is to get back a mass of them. I have a theory as to why, and it has to do with the fact that CEOs and C-suite executives usually don't notice granular movements within a company but do notice trends. In other words, even though it's a totally incorrect way to think, most CEOs don't mind losing one customer. They get over it quickly and don't bother devoting a ton of resources to fixing that one customer's problem, if they devote any at all. But when they see a wave of people leaving, that's a downward trend on a graph, and CEOs *hate* downward trends on graphs. They have to explain downward trends on graphs to their boards of directors, and that's what leads to newspaper headlines like "CEO of XYZ Company Steps Down to Focus on Family." That's code for "CEO Just Got a Boot in the Ass and Is Being Shown the Door."

The key to winning back a herd of defecting zombies is to get a jump on the problem before it's too late—and that means making sure your different departments are talking to each other.

Example: Let's say you work in the customer service department of a baby stroller company. Whether online or on the phone, you talk to customers every day, solving problems, explaining how the strollers fold up (as a parent of a 17-month old, can I encourage baby stroller companies to please make it easier?), and, in general, listening to the occasional complaint and trying to fix the situation.

Over the course of a week, you notice an incremental rise in the number of complaints about a specific problem with a specific type of stroller. As you document all of these complaints, you realize that this really is a thing—and it's only going to get worse.

In most companies, you'd fill out some kind of form for each one. Over time, these forms may or may not make it to another department that, if its staffers have a second, will look to see if there are any trends forming. (Crazily enough, this is how multimillion-dollar product recalls actually get started.)

By the time someone realizes this really is a thing, the masses are revolting (why no, sir, I wouldn't call them revolting . . . perhaps mildly unattractive), message boards and social media are lighting up like Christmas trees, and thousands of Zombie Loyalists now feel scorned. Even if you *could* talk to them all at once to make them realize how sorry you are and how you're going to fix the problem, it wouldn't matter—you've lost them.

That's how it normally works.

But what if, the moment you started to notice the trend, you had the power to pull someone from marketing, someone from engineering, someone from corporate, and someone from PR all into a meeting, in real time, that very day, to discuss what you've found? What if you could get the ball rolling *before* it became a thing? What if you could be proactive and save your zombies before they recovered? Well, then . . . you've avoided a major disaster, you've kept your zombies loyal, and maybe, just maybe, with your stellar wit and smooth, grace-under-pressure thinking, you've converted a few more customers into Zombie Loyalists. *That's* what companies should be doing. We're going to learn how to talk to each other in chapter 8.

So here's a bad joke:

Did you hear about the Zombie with nothing to do? Yeah, he was bored to death.

I know. That's a horrible joke. Give me a break, I'm 9 hours into a 14-hour flight to Tokyo, and I'm starting to go a little loopy here. But the thing to remember is this: Zombies do occasionally get bored. Let's face it: Like everyone, Zombie Loyalists crave attention and love when good things happen to them. And the whole reason they're Zombie Loyalists to your brand, as opposed to another brand, is because you go out of your way to treat them well. But over time, over the constant "regular," day-in and day-out of simply existing, even going out of your way to treat your zombies well, can get, well, boring, for both you and the zombie. What, you don't think the undead crave new things, just like the living? Of course they do.

In chapter 9, we're going to talk about how you can keep your zombies from getting bored—how you can remain top of mind in their worlds, so that even when they're not buying from you at that moment, they still remember you exist.

I might not be thinking about bacon 24/7, but when Oscar Mayer sends me a bacon-scented alarm clock for my iPhone, you know darn well that I'm going to remember to buy Oscar Mayer the next time I go to the store with a craving.

We'll touch on new and different ways of making your audience remember you, including how Virgin Airlines made a one-month-old daughter of a very frequent flier its "youngest elite traveler ever" and how one of NASA's Mars vehicles sent a tweet to say hi to a visitor at the Jet Propulsion Laboratory in California.

We'll talk about hacks you can implement right now, both on your business and on your Zombie Loyalists, to make sure that even when they're not thinking about you, they're thinking about you. In the end, as I mentioned, it's about staying "top of mind." You'll learn how Barry Diller did it when he was president of a Hollywood movie studio and what you can learn from him, 40 years after he did it.

The best part about chapter 9 is that almost every single one of these hacks costs nothing but can reap tons of benefits. A soup chain reached out to someone who posted that she was freezing and mentioned where she was. "My building doesn't believe in heat," she said. The soup chain responded with "Well, maybe they'll believe in soup—How many people in your office? We'll be right up." And brought soup to them. For no reason at all other than to be nice. It was the quickest mass Zombie Loyalist infection of 14 office workers you've ever seen in your life.

And finally, we arrive at chapter 10, the last chapter in *Zombie Loyalists*. Here's where we focus on what we've learned in the previous chapters and how best to implement all the knowledge bombs we've just acquired.

We're going to wrap up with the understanding that Zombie Loyalists are real. They exist, and their existence can either help you grow your business to new heights you've never even imagined or destroy your business in a heartbeat, vanquishing all you've worked for to the four corners of the universe, without so much as a memory that you ever walked the face of the earth.

So . . . knowing that, I encourage you to come along on this ride. If you're still reading this in a bookstore, just walk to the counter and buy the book already. Seriously. I believe it'll be worth it for you.

The end result of your reading this book should be to increase revenue, increase sales, and gain tons of loyal customers who live only to buy from you and tell everyone else why they should buy from you too. If you don't get that out of this book, then I've failed you. But I hate failing, so it's my belief that you'll benefit from this book. Either way, I want to hear from you, and I want your thoughts on what you're reading, whether now or any time over the course of this book. So here's how to reach me:

Email: peter@shankman.com
Twitter: @petershankman
Facebook: http://facebook.com/petershankman
LinkedIn: http://linkedin.com/in/petershankman

Have at it. If nothing else, I promise you this: I always respond. Because, let's face it, that's what a Zombie Loyalist would want.

Welcome to the Zombie Customer Service Revolution. Your training begins now.

2

IDENTIFYING THE BARRIERS TO ZOMBIE LOYALTY

Wall? Zombies will walk around it. Gate? They'll crawl under it. Zombies don't quit until they get what they want, whether brains or customers.

Next to a cat I took in from the streets 13 years ago, I would think that Zombie Loyalists are probably the most loyal creatures out there.

—Me

So you finished chapter 1 and you're still here. You don't think I'm completely insane (yet), and you get the concept of what a Zombie Loyalist is and, more important, how breeding an army of them can launch your business into the stratosphere.

Well, then . . . welcome to the fight, my friend. We're glad to have you, and we welcome you to the small but growing number of businesspeople who understand that now, more than ever before, customer service is what drives revenue, growth, and positive brand awareness. You're in the right place, fighting the good fight.

But if you want to win, you need an army. In this chapter, I'm going to explore with you the top mistakes companies make that prevent them from becoming Zombie Loyalist breeding grounds. Simply put, you're going to learn how to make your company all about the customer.

PROBLEM 1: YOUR COMPANY LOOKS AT CREATING ZOMBIE LOYALISTS AS A "PROJECT" AS OPPOSED TO A LIFE MISSION

Remember the scene in *The Sopranos,* where Tony makes Christopher a full-fledged member of the family? He tells him that there's no going back after this. If he's in, he's in for life, and he's not out until he's dead.

Same thing is true here. You can't half-ass this—Zombie Loyalists can be your most valuable business commodity, but they can also turn on you and destroy you if given a reason. You can't delegate a team to this for a specified time, nor can you put a few people on the "ZL project."

If you want to create a Zombie Loyalist breeding ground, you have to get the entire company on board, and I mean *the entire company*. Every employee, from the front-desk receptionist to the head of marketing, from the vice president of engineering to the chief executive, needs to understand that they're going to be living in a culture of the customer and that without everyone on board, the breeding ground will fail.

We all know about the "customer experience" at Zappos. (If you don't, I recommend you read *Delivering Happiness* by my friend Tony Hsieh.)

What you may not know is that Zappos offers new hires $2,000, no strings attached, to quit within the first 90 days of employment if they don't believe they fit into the company culture.

Think about that for a second: You hire someone, you train them, you invest resources in them, and then you offer them the opportunity of getting a payout to leave. Sounds crazy, until you think about the reason behind it.

Zappos has a *culture of service*. It permeates everything the company does. It's a culture that turns all customers into Zombie Loyalists, from the moment they hit the website until the moment their shoes arrive at their homes. The entire company is focused on creating a breeding ground for the Zappos Zombie Loyalist army, and they know that it's the most important part of their business.

See, if amazing and wowing the customer isn't the most important part of your business, every single day, you'll never create the loyalists you need. You might have the occasional lone zombie who loves you, but you'll never have a 300-type army of Zombie Loyalists ready to spread the word, bring others in, and even fight for you.

LESSON: So Rule 1 of building an army is to get your entire company to understand that *nothing is more important than the customer.* Not profits, not logistics, not execution, nothing. The customer simply has to be the reason each employee comes to work in the morning. That hard-core, laserlike focus on service is what turns a simple customer into a Zombie Loyalist. Every employee must have the same mind-set: I'm here for the customer.

I was giving a talk a few months ago on the topic of customer service, and someone questioned how customers could be more important to the CEO than profits. I simply turned the question around: Where do the profits come from?

See, there will always be people in your company who believe that its strength comes from money, or reputation, or anything but the customer. They'll fight you on it, and the fights will sound like this:

- "Brand awareness is the most important thing to our company, because without brand awareness, no one will know who we are."
- "Marketing and promotion are the most important things to our company, because people need to know we do X."
- "Quality control is the most important thing to our company, because without it, customers won't like our products."
- "Logistics is the most important thing to . . ."

You get the idea. The thing is, though, you're all technically on the same side. You're all fighting *to improve the customer experience.* The sooner the company learns that, the better off you'll all be. So in case you're wondering, the correct response to any of these arguments is that it has to come back to the customer.

- Brand awareness comes from advertising, sure—but the most *believable* brand awareness comes from current customers sharing our story because they were amazed by how they were treated.
- Marketing and promotion are definitely important, but how believable will any ad really be if the first thing a

person sees on Twitter is a host of tweets with the hashtag #yourcompanysucks?

- Quality control is important, definitely, because a great product makes the customer happy, and the customer can tell our story much more believably than we ever could.

Back toward the beginning of my career, I spent a year working for the New Jersey Devils. They had a placard in the locker room above the door that the players skated through to get onto the ice. It read simply:

GOOD ISN'T GOOD ENOUGH, WHEN BETTER IS EXPECTED.

This was a direct quote from Lou Lamoriello, the president and general manager of the Devils, leveled at the New Jersey Sports and Exposition Authority (NJSEA), when the two organizations were negotiating for a new lease for the Meadowlands Arena in 1995. Lamoriello argued that the NJSEA had made only the most minimal efforts to provide the services for which the Devils had contracted under the lease.

Subsequently, Lamoriello had this quote printed above the door. The players saw it every time they left the locker room to go out onto the ice. They lived it as a team, they believed it as a team, and it helped them win games. And as you know, winning teams tend to draw more fans (customers) to their games.

What can you do, today, to help your employees live by the credo that it's always about the customer above *all else?*

PROBLEM 2: YOUR COMPANY DOESN'T COMMUNICATE WELL INTERNALLY

If you can't talk to each other, you can't breed Zombie Loyalists.

A friend of mine, call him James, worked for several years for the head office of a chain of fast-casual restaurants. At this company, few people ever talked to anyone outside of their departments. They all did their own jobs reasonably well, but if they needed more than one department in on a project, they sent memos.

Management thought it was being smart by requiring everyone to document everything, but in actuality, it was hurting the company. By requiring such a rigid communication structure, management actually prevented the company from handling problems naturally and adapting to new ways of business.

"I don't think my company was anticustomer," James told me, "but they certainly didn't make it a priority. When I'd hear a complaint from the outside, I wasn't empowered to fix it without jumping through a million different hoops even if I knew exactly what to do to make the customer happy, and it drove me crazy."

First, James had to email the department responsible for whatever the customer was complaining about. Then he had to wait for a response. This was required by the company, according to James, for "legal reasons," which were never fully explained to him.

Once James got the reply, he had to bring the legal department into the email chain and wait for an answer there. More often than not, the legal team had follow-up questions, further delaying any response from the company to the customer, if one ever came at all.

Think about it for a second: We live in a world where I can order a cheeseburger to my apartment via my mobile phone and return an Amazon delivery for any reason without having to ever speak to a human being. If, thanks to 24-hour customer service and the Internet that never closes, we as customers are being more and more conditioned to expect a response in a "sane" amount of time, if not immediately, what could possibly be the life expectancy of a company that lets customers hang for days or weeks without an answer? The company James worked for is still in business, but it consistently languishes near the bottom of its industry, with no signs of improving. My friend James, however, has since moved on, seeing that nothing was going to change within the company anytime soon.

LESSON: Zombie Loyalist breeding grounds require immediate communication from all parties within a company as well as any and all vendors or outside sources that company uses. From the CEO all the way down to the receptionist, everyone needs to have access to everyone else; every department needs to be connected to every other department.

Have you ever seen a zombie press the "walk" button and then patiently wait for the light to change? Of course not. Zombies don't wait. Zombie Loyalists don't either. Giving them the answer they need, when they need it, is critical to maintaining Zombie Loyalty. Zombies don't care why you haven't responded to them; they only care that you haven't. If the reason is because your company can't get out of its own way and talk to each other, then the problem isn't your customers—it's your company.

PROBLEM 3: EMPLOYEES DON'T UNDERSTAND THEY HAVE THE POWER TO CHANGE THINGS WITHIN THE COMPANY FOR THE BETTER

That doesn't mean anyone can do anything without authorization, but all employees need to know that they have the blessing of management to attempt to improve the customer experience or at least start a discussion about whether it can be done.

The summer before my freshman year of college, I worked for a yogurt shop in Manhattan, one of those chains that were everywhere in the mid- to late 1980s, like Starbucks today. The awning above the entrance was supported by two long brass poles, and they were the dirtiest things you've ever seen. I don't think they'd ever been cleaned, and they didn't shine at all like brass was supposed to.

One slow day, about a half hour before closing, I found some brass polish in the storage room. I took a rag and went outside and starting buffing the hell out of those two poles. I was about a third of the way through the first pole when the franchise owner of the store came outside, asking me why I wasn't behind the counter.

I told him that I thought if the poles shone like they were supposed to, perhaps they would catch the eyes of more people, who would then come in to buy some frozen yogurt.

The owner responded with that classic line that no 17-year-old hourly employee ever wants to hear: "I don't pay you to think. Get back behind the counter."

Well, that shut me down right quick, and it was a good thing I was leaving for college in two weeks, because that was my last day there. I didn't mind getting yelled at, I didn't even mind that I was, to my boss, nothing more than a yogurt dispenser. What really got me was that I truly believed I was doing something that would help the company. Even though I was making minimum wage, I had an idea (a simple one, sure, but an idea), and my reward for taking the initiative? "Shut up, kid. You're an idiot."

LESSON: If your company doesn't allow you to take the initiative—heck, if your company doesn't *reward* you for taking the initiative to try to make things better—you'll never create Zombie Loyalists, because employees will rarely go out of their way to help customers. Why should they? What's in it for the employees? Nothing. If you find yourself recognizing this situation in your company, your options are simple: Change the mentality of the company or find a new job, because a company that doesn't empower employees to help improve that company won't be in business for very long.

PROBLEM 4: COMPANY EXECUTIVES PUT IN PLACE PROCEDURES DESIGNED ONLY TO COVER THEIR ASSES INSTEAD OF PROCESSES DESIGNED WITH THE CUSTOMER IN MIND

Let's talk about banks for a second.

- They exist because they're usually safer than keeping your life savings under your mattress.
- They charge ridiculous fees for every single thing unless you're some kind of millionaire.
- When you think "amazing customer service," you rarely think "bank."

- Most people think their bank sucks, but they don't change banks because they believe that all banks suck.

Back in 2002 or so, I was in the same boat. I was using a big bank that rhymed with the word "mace" and would watch, week by week, as my ATM withdrawals, checks I wrote, or even deposits I made all came with hefty fees that ate into what meager savings I had at the time.

Then one day I was at said bank to deposit a check, and I happened to have my joint dog with me. (A joint dog is one that you adopted from a shelter when you were in a relationship with someone, and when the relationship ended, you stayed friends, and now you both coparent the dog.) As I walked in and got in the long line for the one teller working that afternoon, a manager came out of nowhere to inform me that I had to leave because, unless my dog was a service dog, it wasn't allowed in the bank.

Actual conversation between the bank manager and myself:

"Sir, you need to remove your dog from here, it's not allowed to be here."

"I'm depositing a check, he's on a leash, he's sitting next to me, half asleep. What's the problem?"

"Sir, the bank has a firm policy that no dogs are allowed. You can tie him up outside and come back in."

"I can tie him up outside? We're not on a farm, this is Twenty-third Street in Manhattan. I'm not tying my dog up outside where anyone could steal him and then coming back in and waiting in this line again."

"Then, sir, you can't bank with us today. Our rules are very clear; your dog may bite someone."

At that point, the bank manager motioned for the bank security guard to come over, just in case I put up a fight.

This becomes even *more* ridiculous when you actually see the dog. It's a Labrador-poodle mix. Yes. A Labradoodle. Just typing the word here makes me less manly. I don't ever recall opening up the

local paper and seeing the headline "Cops Break Up Vicious Labradoodle Dog-Fighting Ring." The only thing this dog would ever do to someone is lick them to death, and even that would happen only if he actually bothered to wake up first.

So I walked my vicious, man-eating Labradoodle out of the bank. As I was standing on the corner in complete amazement that the bank I'd been with for over ten years, the bank that had made thousands upon thousands of dollars in fees off me, had just kicked me out for having what was essentially a damn Muppet at my feet, I happened to look across the street and see a brand-new bank that had just entered the New York market, Commerce Bank (now called TD Bank).

Just for kicks, I walked across the street with my check and ventured inside.

Before I'd taken so much as three steps toward the desk, a manager appeared out of nowhere again. (Seriously, where do banks keep their managers that they can just *appear*, like they're the Blair Witch or something?)

But this time, it was different. The manager had this huge smile on her face, and before she even said anything to me, she was on her knees, handing out belly-rubs and ear-scratches.

(It occurs to me here that I should make it clear that the manager was on her knees handing out those things to the dog, not to me.)

As I watched in amazement, another bank employee came over with a Commerce Bank–branded dog biscuit. A freaking *dog biscuit!* She asked if she could give it to my dog and also asked how she could help me.

In my shock over the complete and utter difference between my bank and this one, I simply asked if it would be possible to open up an account, even though I had my dog with me. The reply, of course, was "Of course you can! Why would it matter if you had your dog with you?"

See, Commerce Bank knew that it was opening up in New York City, one of the most dog-friendly cities in the world. Its bank rule for dogs was simple: As long as it's on a leash, it's welcome in our bank. *The bank rule favored the customer while still satisfying the legal minds that drew up the rules in the first place.*

This bank employed logic.

In five minutes, I'd opened up a new account at Commerce Bank. The next day, sans Labradoodle, I went to my now-former bank and pulled my personal checking, corporate checking, personal savings, and corporate savings, taking them all across the street.

End result? I've had over a dozen accounts with TD Bank since 2002, and the bank has made a *lot* more money off of me than my old bank ever did, all because its rules were customer-centric. Oh, and during the summer? TD Bank has doggie bowls filled with water outside every one of its branches, all around the city. I'm a Zombie Loyalist for TD Bank, because it welcomed me *and* my joint dog.

LESSON: If every rule in your company is designed solely to protect it, then it's hard to put the customer first. If the rules are preventing you from breeding Zombie Loyalists, you have a big problem. There's always a middle ground that can protect the company while also making customers feel like they're the most important thing in the world. (Or, at least, their dog is.) Find that middle ground so you please both the customer and management.

PROBLEM 5: COMPANIES THAT REQUIRE EMPLOYEES TO DO EVERYTHING BY THE BOOK WILL NEVER BREED ZOMBIE LOYALISTS

I try not to spend too much time hating things. It's usually a waste of time, and rarely does anything good come from it. But I do reserve a special bit of hate for mobile phone companies.

Let's face it—there's a reason they consistently own the number 1 spot on those "most hated companies" lists you see from time to time. They focus primarily on profits, they make their employees stick to scripts, they offer little to no incentive for customer service agents to think for themselves, and finally, they're completely process and procedure driven, despite reams of evidence proving that even a little leeway would yield a massive uptick in revenue and profits.

I recounted this story on my blog at Shankman.com last year, but it's worth telling again here. I'd just landed in Dubai, in the United Arab Emirates (UAE), for a few speeches and a little bit of desert skydiving and exploring. Before I'd left, I called Verizon Wireless, saying that I was going overseas and to please activate the "Global Roaming" feature on my phone. If you ask a company to do this, you wind up paying about $20 per every 100 megabytes of data that you use. It's not as cheap as it would be if Verizon wasn't run by greedy, profiteering, mean people, but it's better than nothing, and if it means I can turn on my phone when I land on the other side of the world and still get my email, it's worth it to me.

So I land in Dubai and turn on my phone. I see the wireless signal, and I wait for my emails to load. As they do, I receive a text message from Verizon: "You've accumulated over $50 in global roaming charges."

You need to understand: *I hadn't even gotten off the plane yet.*

As I'm scratching my head trying to figure that one out, another text: "You've accumulated over $100 in global roaming charges."

Again, still on the plane.

After getting through immigration and while waiting for my driver, I did what I loathe to do and called Verizon back. And sure enough, "Carl" was nice enough to tell me the following: "Oh, yeah, sorry, sir, but your plan only works in certain countries. Dubai isn't [in] one of them."

I don't know what angered me more—that Verizon assumes that Americans travel only to Mexico and Canada, or that no one ever bothered to tell me that the roaming plan wasn't truly global. Essentially, Verizon's "Global Roaming" plan would have been better named "Hemispherical Roaming."

That's it. Time to fight back. I got to my hotel about 8 p.m. and, after dropping my bags, jumped in a cab to the Dubai Mall. Once there, I found an electronics store that carried every phone known to man. I picked up the Samsung Galaxy Grand for $350 (the Note II in America) and then walked to the Du store (equivalent of Verizon in Dubai). There, for $100, I bought a 25-gigabyte SIM card that works all over the UAE.

So for $450, I now had an unlocked, global mobile phone I could take all over the world, and 25 gigabytes of data. That's it. No other charges, no hidden fees.

A week later, as I got on board my flight to go home, I looked at my new phone's data usage. Over six days in Dubai, I'd used 1,516 megabytes, or about 1.3 gigabytes of data. I had no additional charges, I still have over 23.5 gigabytes left for my next trip, and, most important, Verizon didn't get a *penny* of that.

If I hadn't checked my phone and just taken Verizon at the word of the initial rep who put global on my phone and told me it was "all good" (her words), I'd have come back to America to find a Verizon Wireless bill waiting for me to the tune of more than $31,047.68. Yup. That's not a joke. Do the math yourself: $20.48 per *megabyte*.

The worst part of all of this for Verizon (other than the fact that I use my international phone now whenever I go overseas, and Verizon never sees a dime) is that *it didn't have to be this way.*

Had Verizon had policies in place that empowered Carl to say "Okay, Mr. Shankman, I can do this for you—I'll charge you $500 for a week in Dubai, as long as you don't go over two gigs of data. That cool?" I would have gladly paid it. (Heck, I would have paid double that.) And more important, I would have told the *world* how awesome Verizon was to work with.

Verizon had a spectacular chance to breed me into a new Zombie Loyalist right there on the spot, one who would have shared his story with other business travelers and definitely brought Verizon more revenue. Instead? They blew it. The company's inability to trust its employees to do the right thing for the betterment of the company cost it a lot of money, a lot of current and future business, a lot of loyalty, and a lot of positive brand awareness.

LESSON: If your company puts rules before people and inflexibility before logic, you have a problem. Zombie Loyalists can't breed without flexibility, logic, and trust. If your company doesn't have those, you need to focus on making changes, or you'll never get your zombies to breed.

PROBLEM 6: IF YOUR EMPLOYEES ARE SCARED TO TRY SOMETHING NEW, THEY CAN'T CREATE ZOMBIES

To create a Zombie Loyalist breeding ground for your customers, every single employee must be empowered to thrill, excite, and amaze every single customer, and all employees *must* know that they will never get in trouble or lose their job for attempting to do this.

Ritz-Carlton does it, as does Four Seasons. But so does Claudio Pizzeria Ristorante on 43rd Street and Tenth Avenue, as does Strand Hong Cleaners in Midtown and the In and Out Burger two blocks from Los Angeles International Airport.

Verizon, as I mentioned, doesn't do it. Neither did that yogurt shop back in the 1980s, nor does the deli/grocery on the corner of 13th and Walnut in Philadelphia.

Of course, I'm talking about fostering an environment of empowerment in your company, one that lets employees do whatever they need to do to make a customer happy.

According to an Accenture Consulting study that came out in 2012, 66 percent of customers are willing to spend more money with a company that provides excellent customer service while 85 percent of customers who have left a company said they would have stayed, if only the company had acted differently toward them when they had a problem.[1]

In other words, if all employees at your company don't feel they can take the necessary steps to keep a customer, you'll never breed zombies.

Ever stay at a Ritz-Carlton? If you have, you know how amazing the service is. Why? Because *every single employee,* from a housekeeper to the general manager, has the ability, in real time, to fix a customer's problem, whatever it may be. Whether it's a stuffed toilet or a parent who's on business and needs a one-of-a-kind toy for their daughter back home, every lady and gentleman (as all of the employees at Ritz-Carlton are called) has the power to make your wish come true. As we get deeper into the book, we're going to go into how to do that, and we'll hear from Ritz-Carlton employees themselves, but know this for now: If your company doesn't let every single employee go out of their way to be awesome to every single customer, every single time, you'll never breed the Zombie Loyalists you want in your customers. And here's why:

When people have a problem, they want help. They want the problem fixed, and the person who does that becomes their hero. On the flip side, if the person they ask for help can't fix their problem (or, worse, *won't* fix their problem), that person becomes the goat. And you know what happens to goats? They wind up vilified on the Internet.

LESSON: Remember what we said in the opening chapter? The Internet is powered by two things: bragging and drama. Your brand can grow from bragging, but it is always vulnerable to drama. Having employees who will go out of their way to be Superman for your customers? That's growth via bragging. The opposite? Not fixing a problem? Not being empowered to do so? That turns into drama. Drama can kill your company, and, at the very least, it will kill your Zombie Loyalist breeding plans.

PROBLEM 7: IF YOUR EMPLOYEES REMOVE THEIR "CUSTOMER HAT" WHEN THEY COME TO WORK, THEY CAN'T BREED ZOMBIE LOYALISTS

It's imperative that all employees understand their customers' mentality.

I was driving to Atlantic City to give a speech not long ago and stopped to get gas. New Jersey is one of two states, along with Oregon (and the town of Huntington, Long Island—no, seriously) where it's illegal for drivers to pump their own gas. So naturally, a gas attendant came over and did what I could have easily done myself. While the gas was pumping, she proactively took it upon herself to clean my windows. I was so shocked that I gave her a tip. I can't remember that *ever* happening to me before. But in the 1950s, such service and tips were standard.

Today's standards of service stink. I'll go on record to say that for the most part, customer service falls into two categories: "We suck" and "We only sort of suck." We've gotten used to a lot of bad service practices, and the worst part is that our typical expectation for a customer service transaction starts at poor and, if we're lucky, ends at fair. Even worse, service agents themselves seem to have forgotten how frustrating it is to be that customer who just wants help. Surely, in their own interactions with the businesses they themselves patronize, they'd want better.

The good news is, since we have such universally low expectations of customer service, it's incredibly easy to blow each and every one of your customers' minds and shock them into 100 percent loyalty every single time you're given the chance.

All you have to do is simply make sure you and your team treats each customer exactly as they would want to be treated if they were on the other side of the table. Amazingly, you don't even have to be anywhere near great. Anything we do that goes beyond one level above crap is so rare, and so unexpected, that if you do that, you can rule the world.

A study published in the *Harvard Business Review* found that most customers encounter loyalty-eroding problems when they engage with customer service, with scary stats like these: 56 percent of consumers report having to reexplain an issue; 57 percent report having to switch from the Web to the phone; 59 percent report being transferred to another person because the first person was useless (useless!); and 62 percent report having to contact the company repeatedly to resolve an issue.[2]

LESSON: When we expect, as customers, to be treated like crap in every interaction, it's not hard to train employees to be better than crap. One level above crap keeps customers; two levels and above breeds them into Zombie Loyalists. Strive for this. At the very least, make the company strive to create service that's good. Great is awesome, too, but good is still better than the majority of what we expect today.

PROBLEM 8: IF THE CEO, OWNER, OR HEAD CHEESE CAN'T SHOW EVERY EMPLOYEE THAT BREEDING ZOMBIES COMES FROM THE TOP DOWN AND PERMEATES THE COMPANY, YOU'LL NEVER BREED ZOMBIE LOYALISTS

If you've read my previous book *Nice Companies Finish First,* these next few paragraphs will look familiar to you. In fact, the story I'm about to share about a CEO reaching out to me personally is one of the key events that caused me to coin the term "Zombie Loyalist."

A couple of years ago, I received an email from John Korff, who at the time was the president of Korff Enterprises (otherwise known as the guy who runs the company that puts on the wildly popular New York City Triathlon every summer). Korff's been producing this race since the very beginning, well over ten years ago, when it was ever so small. Now it's one of the yearly crown jewels of the New York City sports world, right up there with the New York City Marathon.

At first I assumed it was a form letter, since I'd been accepted into my eighth triathlon. Why so many? Because I'm an idiot who never learns . . . but I digress. I double-clicked to find an actual email, from John Korff himself, congratulating me for getting in again this year and thanking me for doing my eighth one. I was still pretty sure it was a form letter—customer relationship management software can easily know those things. But still, it was a nice touch.

Either way, I happened to be sitting in front of my computer when it came in, so I dropped a reply back almost immediately, thanking Korff for the note and letting him know that I was also doing the New York City Ironman the following month. I didn't expect a reply, since I still kind of thought I was writing to an auto-email.

Two minutes later: "Wow, Peter—Both! You know, we call those who do the New York City Triathlon then the Ironman the next month 'Hudson Doublers!'" So it actually *was* him. At 6:55 p.m. on a Tuesday night.

What made him email me? Was he looking for repeat "customers," as it were? Those who've done his race more than once? If so, smart—remember, it's not cheap to run these races. Perhaps he realized that and wanted to let us know that our continued support of what he built hadn't gone unnoticed. Perhaps he was just *that* nice of a guy. Perhaps it was all planned out on a spreadsheet, and it was just my time to get that email.

It doesn't matter. I've run a ton of races, all over the place, and this was the first time any race director reached out to thank me, unprovoked, on his own. You can damn well bet I'm going to run his race every year, as long as my body will let me. Another thing that's important to mention. It's not just that Korff is good at sending out emails. His races are very well managed, paragons of efficiency and organization. I've never gotten pissed off at a race because the staff screwed up—they do things simply and they do them right.

LESSON: Again, it's the little things. And when employees notice a CEO taking the time to do the little things—not farming them out, not issuing a memo, not giving the task to a subordinate, but actually doing them—they feel empowered to do the same themselves. Empowered employees breed Zombie Loyalist customers.

PROBLEM NINE: ZOMBIE LOYALISTS CAN'T BREED IN BUSINESSES WITH EMPLOYEES THAT DON'T ACTIVELY LISTEN TO THEIR CUSTOMERS, BECAUSE IF YOU'RE NOT LISTENING, YOU WON'T HAVE CUSTOMERS

Let's use email as an example: Absolutely nothing drives me crazier (and gets me to unsubscribe to a newsletter or quit a business faster) than not being able to read it because I'm on my Android or iPad and not in front of a regular computer with a regular email client.

QUESTION: If you have customers reading your email, your tweets, your Facebook postings, or your blog, why would you go out of your way to annoy them and get them to unsubscribe or turn away? Chances are, you wouldn't, yet people do this every day. They use Flash graphics as the first page of their site, and anyone on a device other than the latest laptop can't go past that page.

They use tons of high-resolution graphics in an email, not realizing that countless people are reading their email on a Droid in a land of minimal coverage.

They make the links hard to find or read, or, worse, make people scroll all the way to the bottom to find them. (Ever have to scroll through ten pages of text on a mobile? I'd rather chop off my thumbs.)

LESSON: If your company causes grief to the very people who pay your bills, your company won't breed Zombie Loyalists.

Four Quick Thoughts on Content
1. You don't control how customers get content. *They* do.
2. Before you do your first reach-out to the customer, know exactly how they like to receive their information. Just

because you have all of their contact info doesn't mean you have the right to use it. (Try to sell me something by calling my mobile, and I'll crush you.)

3. Just knowing that they like to receive your content a certain way doesn't cut it. Email? Great. What type? An email on a desktop is a much different experience from an email on a mobile device. There's a reason text-based emails haven't gone away.

4. If your audience isn't where you're trying to reach it, you won't reach it. Sounds simple, but way too many companies have yet to figure this out.

Keep it simple. When you send out your emails, confirm that people want to receive them that way. Text only? Make sure you have a backup version that sends only text, and make sure you offer people the option to receive it that way.

I once had a client who, instead of asking his customers how they wanted to be communicated with, simply said, "But everyone will have full html email on all devices in the next year." This was four years ago. How's that going? Even if customers did have full html email, which they don't, it doesn't mean it will look good, nor does having it equate to ease of use.

Businesses that don't actively listen can't breed zombies. Only companies that take the time to listen, process feedback, and actively make changes based on what they learn will ever create Zombie Loyalists.

PROBLEM 10: IF YOUR COMPANY DOESN'T REALIZE THAT EVERY SITUATION IS DIFFERENT AND EVERY CUSTOMER HAS A DIFFERENT STORY TO TELL—AND INSTEAD TREATS EVERYONE THE SAME—YOU'LL NEVER CREATE ZOMBIE LOYALISTS

Another plane story: I watched an amazing experience one morning at the United counter at LaGuardia. I wasn't in line; I was leaning against a wall tweeting something before I went through security.

Someone showed up in obvious distress. As far as I could tell, the cab driver had taken her to Kennedy when she meant to go to LaGuardia, and, of course, she missed her flight. She said something to the effect of "the person on the phone said I'd have to pay hundreds of dollars in change fees to get onto the next flight, and I can't afford it. Can you please help me get home?"

As far as I could tell, the agent at JFK told her there was nothing he could do, and she should go back to LaGuardia and plead her case. So she did. The gate agent took a look at the ticket, typed some magic into the keyboard, and presented her with a boarding pass for a flight to Chicago, where she could connect to a flight to her city that would get her in a few hours later than her original itinerary.

She presented her credit card to the agent, and I could feel her distress. In this economy, for a lot of people, an extra $300 to $400 in change fees is a huge, huge burden, even if the mistake was entirely the passenger's fault.

The ticket agent smiled and said, "Don't worry about it, the fees are waived. Your flight leaves in fifty minutes."

You should have seen the change in this woman. She went from crying to ecstatic.

She reached over and bear hugged the agent, almost strangling her in the process. She hugged random people next to her. She jumped up and down. She started crying again, this time out of happiness. It was mind-blowing. All she could say was "Thank you, United is so wonderful, I'm going to tell everyone, thank you, thank you, thank you."

It put everyone around her in a better mood as well. People smiled as they made their way to the TSA agents, which never happens. A few people were talking about how unexpected the ticket agent's actions were. "This is why I fly United," said one person.

LESSON: If your company doesn't realize that there are a million stories out there, and each one needs to be dealt with in its own way, you'll never create Zombie Loyalists.

By the way, now's probably a good time to say that I have no relationship with United Airlines or most other companies I mention in this book, other than being a fan of their services and using them frequently. I clearly indicate any company with which I *do* have a financial relationship when I talk about it.

PROBLEM 11: YOUR EMPLOYEES AREN'T BRILLIANT AT THE BASICS

There was once a newspaper editor who told all his reporters to follow one simple rule: "Be brilliant at the basics." For journalists, that meant getting the who, what, when, where, how, and why of the story, always finding the human interest angle, and making sure that everyone who was involved in the story was fairly represented.

In other words, the editor wanted his reporters to shine at the mundane tasks. He believed that only then could they excel at everything else.

If your company has problems being brilliant at the basics—if the most mundane tasks are cause for concern and customers can't interact with your company with confidence over small things—how will customers possibly trust you enough with big things, let alone with their reputation when it comes to recommending you? In other words, you can't breed Zombie Loyalists who will bring you new customers until you master pleasing the customers you already have.

Are there more problems that could prevent your company from breeding? Sure there are, and if you're truly intent on creating Zombie Loyalists, you need to weed them out as well.

But chances are, they're all facets or offshoots of the problems listed in this chapter.

What's the easiest way to prime your company into a Zombie Loyalist breeding ground? Well, if what's preventing you from doing it is process related, try chopping down the process tree.

Each process tree is designed because it does something, right? "If the customer says this, do this, which will result in this." But does it really always work that way? Usually it doesn't.

Can you get management to understand that the current processes are broken or, if not broken, then in desperate need of updating? Can you show them numbers that prove you out?

TIP: People who put rules into place do so because somewhere they have a statistic that says the company will make more money if they do so. But chances are, that's an old stat. Can you show them new stats? Start with this one: 71 percent of customers will leave a company and take their business elsewhere if they encounter inflexible rules that aren't designed to help them. Seventy-one percent! There's not a CEO or bean counter out there who won't shake with fear at that stat, which comes from American Express, by the way.[3]

If you see your company in this chapter, focus first on changing the rules to be more customer-centric. Once you start doing that, your company becomes a fertile breeding ground for creating your customer army of Zombie Loyalists.

Onward!

3

LEADING YOUR COMPANY TO AN OPTIMAL LEVEL OF BREEDING READINESS TO CREATE ZOMBIE LOYALISTS

(OR, HOW TO BUILD A CORPORATE CULTURE THAT LETS ALL EMPLOYEES WORK TO THEIR BEST, HAPPIEST, AND MOST CREATIVE POTENTIAL)

Perhaps you recognized yourself (or your bosses, or your employees) in the previous chapter. If so, good. Identifying the issues and working to fix them is a great start. Chapter 3 picks up where chapter 2 left off, elaborating on how to make sure your company culture is so great that your employees can't help but create Zombie Loyalists with every customer interaction they have.

Let's look at some real examples from companies around the world that have turned their customers into Zombie Loyalists. The one commonality in all these companies?

The core tenet of each is that they value their employees. They value them, they respect them, they go out of their way to make their employees' lives better.

Only when a company treats their employees as their most important asset can the employees treat their customers the same way.

IF EMPLOYEES FEEL VALUED, CUSTOMERS HAVE A MUCH BETTER CHANCE OF FEELING VALUED AS WELL

Open-door policies, or simply walking around and talking to your employees, work wonders in small to mid-size businesses. Managers who take a proactive interest in their employees' well-being tend to have happier, more productive employees. This can be as simple as letting an employee know that you're always available to talk, long before a problem arises.

When I worked in the newsroom at America Online back in the 1990s, I had a boss named Dean Wheeler. Dean would always say that his door was open for anything we might want to talk about.

Sure enough, when we saw the beginnings of a problem, we went to Dean before it became a real problem.

Because we felt valued, because we trusted Dean, we naturally resolved issues that would have cost real money if left to fester for weeks or months. It wasn't rocket science. It was human nature. Dean was one of my favorite bosses, and I was loyal to him until he passed away several years ago.

LESSON: If your business culture is closed off or heavily siloed, you're going to have a very hard time creating Zombie Loyalists. If you want your customers to be loyal, you first need loyal employees. And that comes from the top.

MICROMANAGING EMPLOYEES IS THE FASTEST WAY TO DRIVE AWAY ZOMBIE LOYALISTS

If your company has a culture of micromanaging, you can't breed loyal customers.

Michelle runs an independent garden center, the kind of store that sells everything you need to make your front lawn, back lawn, side lawn, and vegetable garden look amazing, from seeds, to plant food, to gnomes. I live in New York City, and I didn't know these stores even existed until I keynoted an annual conference for the Independent Garden Center Association. (Yes, there's an Independent Garden Center Association. Now you know.)

Anyway, Michelle tells the story of her first job working for someone else in their garden center several years ago:

The owner constantly told me I was her best employee, and I never once got in any kind of trouble for doing anything wrong during the two years that I was there, but every day I worked at that garden center was more of a nightmare than the previous one.

No matter what task I was completing, whether I was stacking planting pots or helping a customer, my boss was always there to critique and offer "suggestions" on ways to do it better. The problem is, there really aren't many ways to stack a planting pot, and once you learn the way that works, you don't need any more help on the issue.

Unfortunately, that boss believed that everyone needed help doing everything, and she didn't trust anyone to independently do the jobs for which they were hired. And it just became a totally uncomfortable place to work. By six months in, I was coming in before the boss did and leaving after she left, just so I could get my work done without being corrected by her.

The worst part was that it was affecting customers. She'd come over as I was in the middle of making a sale and ask the customer if I was doing everything to their satisfaction. She interrupted the flow of the sale, and more than a few times, I'd lose the chance to upsell the customer on something I know I could have gotten them to buy.

Some of my regular customers, after a while, would tell me that they were going to stop shopping with us because they couldn't handle how my boss would constantly micromanage the sale. In fact, they were the customers who suggested I go out on my own and start up my own store. I now own two stores, with 12 employees, and I couldn't be happier.

Michelle told me that she believes her former employer loses and has to hire new employees at a rate of about one every three months, yet she won't change her ways.

It seems evident that it costs much more to lose an employee and have to hire and train a new one than it does to keep the ones we have happy. But a surprising number of managers (and owners) *don't* actually realize that, so they keep biting off their noses to spite their faces.

By constantly trying to "help," a manager can easily become overbearing and harm the entire culture of the company. Micromanaging is one of the kisses of death for a happy, productive workforce that's dedicated to breeding Zombie Loyalist customers.

Look, you hired an employee for a reason: He or she has a skill you need that will help you grow your business. So perhaps, if you see yourself in Michelle's description of her boss, maybe it's time to reevaluate how you deal with your employees.

Employees have to be trusted to do the job put in front of them on their own, once they're trained to do it, much like a mother bird eventually has to kick the baby bird out of the nest and trust that it will fly.

If management can't do that, it will never create loyal employees who can breed Zombie Loyalists. Instead, it will create a cycle of codependence and frustration and, eventually, angry employees who leave to find a better place, taking customers with them.

LESSON: Don't micromanage. Hire the right people to do the right jobs, and let them fly free. Help them if they need it, but otherwise, have faith in them to do what you brought them in to do: Grow your business and create Zombie Loyalist customers.

ZOMBIE LOYALIST BREEDING GROUNDS MUST ALWAYS BE OPEN TO NEW IDEAS

As a business trying to create Zombie Loyalists, you have to understand that not trying new things just because they might not work is a guarantee for failure.

There's always a new way to market, a new way to promote your business, a new way to interact with your customers that simply hasn't been tried yet—either because no one's thought of it or, more likely, because someone was afraid of what would happen.

When Samsung decided to showcase the power of the cameras inside its new phones, it gambled big and decided to have a selfie taken during the 2014 Oscars, live, as the show was in progress. It had Ellen DeGeneres, the host, go into the audience and take a photo with Bradley Cooper, Brad Pitt, Angelina Jolie, and several others in real time.

We all know the end result: the selfie tweeted round the world. Millions upon millions of retweets in a matter of minutes, and a huge visibility boost for Samsung and its line of Note and Galaxy phones.

But imagine, for a second, being on the Samsung team as they thought up the stunt. "What if it doesn't work? What if the image is blurry or the lighting is wrong? What if the camera freezes? What if, what if, what if?"

Implementing any idea for your business comes with a few choices: You can worry about it, overthink it, and eventually not do it; you can dismiss it out of hand; or you can give it a shot.

Most businesses spend way too much time worrying and miss countless opportunities for greatness. To create Zombie Loyalist customers, you have to be willing to embrace the fear that comes with new ideas as well as the possibility that, every once in a while, one will fall flat. That's just the nature of business and of creativity. You take the best information you have at the time and make the best decision you can.

LESSON: As they say, fortune favors the bold. Lead your company in a way that allows you to take more calculated risks. Only companies that take these risks can become breeding grounds for Zombie Loyalist customers.

ENHANCE THE LIVES OF EMPLOYEES IN ANY WAY POSSIBLE, BECAUSE HAPPIER, MORE WELL-ROUNDED EMPLOYEES CREATE ZOMBIE LOYALIST CUSTOMERS

There are two kinds of employees in the world: those who love their job and talk it up every chance they get, and those who don't.

Karl Wiedemann is the communication and sponsorship manager for Thule, Inc. Thule makes those cool bike and sport carrying cases you see on the tops of cars, and it also makes luggage, bags, sport bags, and the like. The company truly lives by its motto: "Bring Your Life."

Thule is a very strong proponent of enhancing the lives of its employees on a regular basis, knowing that happier employees produce happier customers as well as make higher-quality products.

They also decrease costs, improve retention rates, and ensure a much stronger and more cohesive culture within the company.

Being a lifestyle company, Thule has an opportunity to attract many talented people with a passion for the outdoors. But keeping those people is a daily challenge. Thule continually works to provide employees with ways to embrace their passions for the outdoors while at work.

A Swedish company, Thule came to the United States in the early 1980s during the windsurfing boom and was one of the first companies to offer a solution to carry the huge boards on cars. In 1992 Thule moved to Seymour, Connecticut, and set up its US headquarters. Today, that factory still makes a majority of Thule's racks and carriers.

"I can't tell you how many people I have given factory tours to who are blown away that we are an international company making products, with solar power, in the Naugatuck Valley of Connecticut with American workers," said Wiedemann. "Of course, US manufacturing is a good thing for the economy, but you would be amazed at what it can do for the sense of pride and goodwill of your employees. The power of word-of-mouth employee pride is one of your company's best assets."

In other words, give your employees something to talk about!

With bike racks being one of Thule's largest product categories, the company has a huge cycling culture. People who don't already ride are encouraged to borrow a bike and join the daily lunch ride.

The large employee bike room is always full. Each day at noon, a group of 20 to 25 people go for an hour-long ride in the hills around the office. Running late for a ride? No need to worry. There is a set route each day so laggards can catch up if they want to. At the end of the ride, Thule provides showers and lockers.

A few years back, some employees were getting into mountain biking. They asked senior management if they could build some trails on site, and management agreed without hesitation. Today, employees can use this trail network to mountain bike, trail run, walk, or snowshoe.

For people who are not into action sports, Thule brings in a yoga instructor twice a week, and there are always people working out to DVDs in the exercise room, running on the treadmills, or riding stationary bikes.

Thule also prides itself in hosting an annual river cleanup that has removed hundreds of tons of trash from the Naugatuck River over the years. The company gives employees the day off from work to participate. After the cleanup, the company hosts a barbecue as a way to say thanks for the help.

Events like this help bring employees together in a fun, relaxed setting so they can bond with others. Nothing builds fast friendship like removing car tires and shopping carts from a river.

Even sales meetings at Thule are anything but boring. For the past few years, they've been held at the Alta Lodge in Utah's Wasatch Mountains. After a morning yoga class to get the blood flowing, typical sales meeting activities take place: presentations, sales programs, and so on. But at the end of the day, employees and sales reps are encouraged to go hiking, road or mountain biking, play volleyball, or go for a run. Sometimes Thule even hosts a dinner that you have to hike to.

All these things are very inexpensive to implement, but the way Thule's employees embrace them keeps them happy, healthy, and working hard.

People spend so much of their lives at work. Why not make it a bit more fun for them and help them share their passions? Thule employees are always talking with customers, suppliers, and consumers about who won the race to the top on a lunchtime climb, the hike they did at the sales meeting, or the yoga class they just got out of.

People outside the office are always happy to hear about it and a bit envious of the culture at Thule. It helps Thule keep an edge on competitors, and makes it a lot easier to empower the employees to breed Zombie Loyalists.

LESSON: When employees see a connection between what they're able to do and learn and grow from *outside* their day jobs and the company for which they work, the company will always be stronger and more cohesive, with a happier and more positive culture. This, of course, not only translates into how customers are treated but also turns employees into *fans* of their company. And fans tend to speak highly of what they love to anyone who will listen.

EMPLOYEES WHO FEEL A STRONG CONNECTION BETWEEN WHAT THEY DO EVERY DAY AND THE OUTPUT THEY'RE CREATING TEND TO DO IT BETTER, WITH LESS DOWNTIME AND FEWER MISTAKES

Show your employees the end result of their work. When I was running my last start-up, Help a Reporter Out (HARO), I would get emails from members every day. HARO allows regular people to get free publicity in the media. It's a simple mailing list with "queries" from journalists all over the world. We sent out emails to over a quarter million people three times a day. When you'd get a HARO email, you'd scan it to see if there was a reporter working on a story about which you were knowledgeable. If there was, you dropped a quick note to the reporter explaining your expertise. If the reporter wanted your info, he or she would email you back, and you'd be interviewed. It was 100 percent easy.

The end result was that you'd get quoted in the paper, or on TV, or featured on the radio, in a news article or blog or something similar.

It was occasionally stressful work, but my team and I loved it. And whenever someone got in the media, they'd email us and tell us about it. (Heck, whenever someone got in the media, they'd email the world and tell them.)

But their stories were always amazing. One woman ran a bakery in the Midwest. She was close to shutting down and laying off her last three employees because the recession hit in 2008 and she lost several key contracts.

The woman was on HARO and happened to respond to a media query from a national newspaper asking about companies that were being hit hard by the recession. Her story, complete with photos of her cakes and baked goods, was featured on the front page of this newspaper. Within three days, she was receiving orders from all over the world, and within two months, she was rehiring the employees she'd had to let go.

Do you have any idea how amazing it made us at HARO feel, knowing we had a part in saving this woman's business and keeping her employees working? It extended outward too—that story, and the business she got from it, helped feed the families of the people who worked for her and helped her town do just a little better by extension. How awesome is that?

I used to take all my employees to lunch each Friday, and we'd read all those types of emails over a meal. It was such a great feeling, and the employees went back to work with an enhanced sense of purpose and meaning. Plus, you know they shared those stories with their friends and anyone who would listen.

By showing my employees how their day-to-day actions were actually impacting the world for the better, I was able to help them enjoy their jobs more, motivate them to work harder, and let them become Zombie Loyalists for their own company as well.

LESSON: Make sure your employees know the value of what they're doing by finding ways to show them the results, whether it's by following up with customers or highlighting specific uses of the product they created or the customer interactions they have. Doing so enables them to want to do great things more often, and that greatness turns customers into Zombie Loyalists.

PERKS DON'T ALWAYS COME IN THE FORM OF MONEY, BUT YOU DON'T NEED TO BUY A CORPORATE TRAMPOLINE EITHER

After HARO was acquired, I spent a few years working for the company that bought us, Vocus, Inc. One of the keys of Vocus's success was that it knew a lot about each employee, even as the company was growing and adding hundreds of new people a year. Management took it upon themselves to learn about each person they brought on board.

One Vocus employee was a competitive swing dancer in her spare time. After a coworker organized a group to watch her compete one night, management got wind of her hobby and proceeded to sponsor an upcoming competition. Why? Because she was a valuable employee, and Vocus knew that swing dancing was important to her.

On the flip side, I have a skydiving friend named Marco who worked for an engineering firm (when he wasn't throwing himself out of planes). Marco is really into wing-suiting (those suits you see in the movies that make people look like flying squirrels) and is always trying to improve on his training.

One day Marco's boss came up to him and offered him use of the company's multimillion-dollar 3-D imaging computer, so he could be "motion-captured" in his wing suit and possibly gain some insights into how to improve his flying to spend more time in the air. Understand, this is not something any skydiver has access to, ever— this is some next-generation space stuff.

Marco was over the moon. What wound up happening? He started spending a lot more time at work, not only for his wing-suit project, but to figure out other uses for this supercomputer that he could apply directly to his clients' projects. It was a double win, both for Marco and for the company.

More and more, research I've done has shown that while employees certainly want to be fairly compensated for their work, the real value in a job for many employees is the feeling that management cares and takes an interest in their lives as a whole.

This doesn't mean you should start snooping on your employees when they're outside the office, but validation goes a long, long way, and little things like what Marco's boss did guarantee employee loyalty, trust, and growth within the company, all traits that lead to employees wanting to turn customers into Zombie Loyalists.

LESSON: You can't fake loyalty, nor is it something you can build half-assed. If you truly want to empower your employees, focus not just on how they do their jobs but rather on helping them to better live their lives.

LOSE ONE CUSTOMER, AND YOUR COMPANY WILL SURVIVE. LOSE ONE EMPLOYEE, AND IT MIGHT NOT

Think about a dog for a second, if you would. I mean, come on, who doesn't love dogs? We could all stand to think about dogs more often.

So, imagine adopting a puppy from a shelter, perhaps just a day or two before he was scheduled to be put down. You bring your new friend back with you and give him a home, shelter, food, warmth, and love. You become friends.

Fast forward about five years. You're sleeping in your bed at 2 a.m. when your dog (now no longer just a little puppy) wakes up to an almost imperceptible sound coming from downstairs. Bounding off the bed, he runs to the top of the stairs, where he sees a burglar who has just jimmied open your front door.

In a mad frenzy of growling and barking, without one iota of fear or hesitation, your dog leaps from the top of the stairs, his incredibly powerful jaws and teeth locking dead onto the burglar's thigh, puncturing the skin and drawing blood. As you wake up and realize what's going on, the burglar is off and running down the street, having dropped his bag and tools in his mad dash to escape.

The police are called and track the blood drops, catching the limping and bleeding burglar just a few blocks away. Turns out, he's robbed several houses in the neighborhood in the past few months, but thanks to the loyalty of your four-legged friend, his burgling days are over.

What made your dog do that? The answer is simple: loyalty. Your dog is 100 percent loyal to you, and nothing in the world will ever change that. Why? Because you are 100 percent loyal to him: You took him in when he was just a puppy. You saved his life. You provide him with food, shelter, care, and love. In return, he loves you unconditionally and will gladly put his life in danger to protect yours.

Employees are no different. I'm not calling employees dogs, of course, but the analogy is sound. Employees who feel that the company for which they work is loyal to them will almost always return that loyalty.

This means that when it comes down to a fight between a customer and an employee, if the employee is in the right, it's the company's job to defend that employee, even if it means losing a customer in the process.

I once "fired" a client of my public relations (PR) firm on the spot, because the client's chief executive spent an entire dinner making rude, inappropriate advances to one of my employees. The employee, a young woman just starting out in the industry, was afraid to make waves or stand up to the client. The second I saw what was going on, I ended our relationship with the client.

That was in February 2000. I'm still good friends with that employee. In fact, she now works for a Fortune 50 bank, and two months ago she brought me in to keynote her annual North American sales conference.

LESSON: Employees need to know that, when push comes to shove, the company will have their backs and protect them. Those who say there's no such thing as corporate loyalty anymore simply haven't been working for the right companies.

MORE RESPONSIBILITY EQUALS HIGHER EMPLOYEE VALUE

A very popular public speaker in the marketing and PR space had a problem. He was getting good speaking gigs around the country but felt like he could be doing more. So he went to multiple speaking agencies looking for representation. He was told time and time again that he wasn't big enough, his niche wasn't big enough, and he wasn't worth the agents' time.

Dejected, he was in his office in Chicago one day, complaining to his assistant about it. He said something to the effect of "Hell, I should let you get me gigs."

The assistant asked him if she could try and get the same commission that he'd give to the big speaking agencies. With nothing to lose, the speaker agreed.

Within two weeks, his assistant had booked him three gigs, each one at a higher rate than he'd ever booked himself.

Why? She'd been given the chance. I asked her what made her go out and work so hard for him, when the speaking agencies wouldn't give him the time of day.

She told me, "I felt that I could do it, but I never had the chance. When I finally got it, I wanted to prove what I could do. I'd heard him speak many times and knew he was good. I was able to take my passion for his talent and express that to the people I called."

In your company, chances are incredibly good that your employees have the talent, ability, and drive to do amazing things, but their hands are tied for one reason or another, or they simply don't know if they're allowed to, or they don't know where to take their ideas. Work toward creating a culture where anyone is empowered to try something new that benefits the company. If they do it and fail, they've learned something, and if they do it and succeed, they're that much stronger for it and that much more loyal for the experience.

LESSON: Letting your employees try builds loyalty and trust within an organization, improving the company culture as a whole.

FAIL OFTEN!

I carry a napkin in my wallet on which I once wrote the words "Fail Often!" I keep it in there to remind me that there's absolutely nothing wrong with failure. In fact, I even have a podcast dedicated to failure and what you can learn from it. It's called "The Mistake Podcast," and you can grab it in the business section on iTunes.

A business where failure is thought of not as a weakness but rather as a positive trait will consistently have a better and more loyal culture than one with an eat-the-weak mentality. If your employees are afraid to fail, then they'll be afraid to try. If you have a workplace where everyone is afraid to try, then you certainly won't create Zombie Loyalist customers. Without embracing failure, some of the greatest customer service stories in the world would never have taken place. (Wait until I share my Morton's Steakhouse story with you later in the book.)

A great story passed down through the years involves the late Tom Watson, Jr., chief executive of IBM in the early 1960s. He called a young executive to his office after the man had lost $10 million in a failed and highly risky venture. As Watson's legendary temper was not a secret, the man assumed he was about to be fired and instead tendered his resignation to the CEO.

"Fire you? You've got to be kidding," Watson is reported to have replied. "Hell, I spent $10 million educating you. I just want to be sure you learned the right lessons."

I've always loved that story. A company that isn't afraid to try and fail will almost always succeed.

LESSON: Create a culture for your business that makes it clear that it's completely okay to try and fail.

IF YOU DON'T WELCOME, EMBRACE, AND EMPLOY CHANGE, YOU'LL NEVER BREED ZOMBIE LOYALIST CUSTOMERS

It's time to whip out my favorite change-needs-to-happen story, one that I've shared in almost every other book I've written. Why? Because it's mandatory reading if you're trying to turn your company into a Zombie Loyalist customer breeding ground.

Simply put, nothing good has ever come without change. Change moved us from horses to cars, change moved us from trains to airplanes. Without change, there'd be no space program, no democracy, no bikinis, nothing. Without change, we wouldn't be here.

Look at companies that have failed due to their inability to embrace change—Kodak, for instance. Polaroid. BlackBerry. Gateway.

All were once great leaders in their space who thought, "We're doing great, we call the shots."

On a scale of "not bad at all" to "let's invade Russia in the winter," not embracing change has to be one of the deadliest moves a company can make.

To succeed in the world of the customer, companies desperately need to embrace change, not fear it. Customers' needs change minute by minute. If you can't keep up, they'll go somewhere else. The key is to be flexible. If you roll with the changes and adapt in real time, your company will be a hero to your customers—and heroes build Zombie Loyalist customers. But if you don't change, you're gone, and so are your zombies.

I used to use Yahoo! as my search engine back in the day. Then Google launched, and it was better. But Yahoo! stuck to its guns, and Google ate its lunch. We see it all the time in tech but also in the rest of the world. Heck, Portugal once had a huge, massive navy. Change came; now it has cheap condos.

Our past is beyond full of people, places, countries, and dynasties that didn't embrace change and found themselves on the losing end of history. If you want to create loyalty, in both your employees and your customers, everyone in your company needs to look at what's coming down the road 5, 10, 20 steps ahead.

Here's my favorite parable about change. I heard it from one of my first bosses in my first job, and it involves baboons. Enjoy.

Week 1: Place six baboons in a room. On the ceiling fan, place a banana. Every time a baboon tries to reach for the banana, spray all the baboons with an ice-cold shower. It doesn't matter who reaches for the banana; all baboons get sprayed. After a week of research, no baboon in the room will attempt to reach for the banana.

Week 2: Take out one of the baboons and introduce a new one to the room. The first thing that the newcomer will try to attempt is to reach for the banana on the ceiling fan. However, he will face great aggression and intimidation from the other baboons, since they, of course, know that the new baboon's attempt will be followed by the ice-cold shower. (In other words, the old baboons will beat the hell out of the new one.) After a while, the newcomer will stop attempting to reach for the banana, since anytime he does so, he's beaten up by five old-timers. He doesn't know *why* he's not allowed to have the banana, just that when he tries to grab it, he winds up in a lot of pain.

Week 3: Take yet another original baboon out of the pack, and introduce a new one. Observe the same scenario. Also, observe the newcomer from Week 2 admonishing the new baboon not to reach for the banana.

Week 4: Same thing. Now you've got three baboons from Week 1 and three new baboons.

Week 5: Same thing.

Week 6: Same thing.

Week 7: This is where it gets interesting. A brand-new baboon is introduced, and none of the original baboons who were in Week 1 remain. In other words, not *one* baboon now in the cage has ever been on the receiving end of an ice-cold shower. However, observe how aggressively the newcomer will be "advised" when he tries to reach for the banana.

So why doesn't any baboon reach for the banana?

Because that's the way they've always done it.

Crazy, huh?

LESSON: Refusing to accept, learn, and grow from change will take down your company and severely impact your ability to breed Zombie Loyalist customers. Also, if you say the word "baboon" enough times, it makes you laugh.

EVERYONE HAS TO DO IT, NO MATTER THE JOB

I'm reminded of a very large company with an even larger call center. It's one of the few companies that doesn't outsource its call centers to another country but keeps them in America to help build jobs.

Anyhow, every person who doesn't work in the call center of this company (i.e., the rest of the company) is required to spend one day every six months shadowing a call-center employee, listening in on the conversations, and even taking a call or two.

A national pizza chain requires their senior executives to spend three days a year taking orders, making pizzas, and going out on delivery runs. A company that makes copper piping and tubing for half the world requires all of its salespeople to work on the factory floor every once in a while.

Why all of this? These companies know that true culture, *unified* corporate culture, can't come from one group of people sitting in an office while another works on the factory floor, both clueless as to what the other does.

Unified corporate culture requires every employee to understand that it's their job to help grow the company. Whatever they do, in whatever division, contributes to the bottom line of the business and determines whether the company has regular old customers or Zombie Loyalist customers.

I once spent a college summer working at a photo lab. (For those readers under 30, to take pictures, you used to have to use a camera, then take something out of the back of the camera called "film," which you'd take to a store to have turned into pictures. It was a whole process, and why most photos you see of your grandparents seem to have been taken only at Christmas and graduations.)

Anyhow, one day, the special photo printing machine went down, and the fix involved draining the dyes and flushing the machine. It wasn't complicated, but it was a big pain, and it made you smell horrible for the rest of the day, regardless of how many gloves or aprons you wore. Each photo store had one person who did this job. The day our printer broke, though, that guy was home sick.

So I volunteered to do it. Why? Because it had to be done. People were expecting to pick up their pictures.

Forty-five minutes later, the printer was back up and running, and you couldn't get within 20 feet of me without wanting to vomit. It never occurred to me not to do it, though.

I'm not a martyr or anything like that, nor am I a suck-up. I just believe that when you're hired to work for a company, the greater good of the company is more important than one person. The nice thing about that logic is that the opposite is true too: If a company is supported by employees who care, the company will support the employees right back. That symbiotic relationship is what allows employees to create Zombie Loyalist customers.

Creating a corporate culture that embraces the it's-my-job philosophy is not easy, but the dividends it pays are well worth it. If I know that I can go to a store and anyone there can help me with my problem, and that no matter how long it takes, it'll get resolved, I'm a Zombie Loyalist to that company for life.

LESSON: All employees in any company need to understand that no job is beneath them, no job is too small, messy, annoying, or smelly, and all employees answer to a higher calling of the company as a whole. That's how Zombie Loyalist customers are bred.

HELP DEVELOP THE EMPLOYEE, AND THE EMPLOYEE WILL HELP DEVELOP THE ZOMBIE LOYALIST

The *NonProfit Times* recently came out with its 2014 "Best Non-Profits to Work For" list, and at number 1 was the National Older Worker Career Center, Inc.[1]

When interviewed, center staff stated over and over again that after a fair salary and benefits, the ability to learn new things and grow their talents were the top loyalty boosters and reasons they loved their jobs.

Makes sense, when you think about it. If you allow your employees to grow while under your roof, they're going to get better and, more often than not, move up within the company instead of moving out to a new company. As long as there's room to grow and places to go, employees in a company that treats them well and has a great culture will rarely leave.

My friend Henry Posner, social media director for B&H Photo, just celebrated 20 years with the company. When I asked him why he's still there, here's what he said:

Respect. I was a customer before I became an employee and already knew they were a kosher joint among the more dubious gang from the back of Pop Photo.

Mutual respect. After a period of them learning to trust me and my accepting the particulars of the B&H and Hasidic cultures (not the same thing, BTW) I always felt included in the decision-making process and always felt I was listened to. I didn't win every argument, but I always had the chance to get my proverbial two cents in.

Ownership. I always felt I was part of our success and never felt my boss was basking in my light or forcing me into his shade.

Independence. I'm difficult to manage and know it, but my boss understood that I could do my job better than he could and in fact he couldn't really do my job at all. As long as I had my priorities in order and my head screwed on straight, I was encouraged and never felt anyone was sitting on my shoulder.

LESSON: Help your employees grow. Zombie Loyalist customers breed much better when they work with the same employee over and over again.

TIME IS EMPLOYEES' MOST VALUABLE RESOURCE. LET THEM USE IT THE WAY THAT BEST WORKS FOR THEM

I never truly understood the value of being able to work from anywhere until I started skydiving.

See, it gets cold in New York City during the winter, and skydiving in cold weather, while possible, simply isn't fun. You're bundled up with tons of layers, you can't fly as free as you want to in the sky, and no matter how warm your gloves are, your fingers still hurt by the time you land. It's much more fun to skydive in warm weather.

Which is why I truly love being able to take a random winter Tuesday and fly someplace warm to spend the next day repeatedly falling from planes.

Fact is, while customer service employees in stores have to actu-ally be on site, others don't. More customer service is done from pri-vate homes, backyards, beaches, or airplanes than ever before, thanks to Wi-Fi, VPNs, and noise-canceling mouthpiece microphones.

The biggest hurdle to allowing employees to work from any-where, however, is a corporate mind-set that they won't get as much done.

I'm not saying let every employee work from a forest in Labra-dor, but if an employee needs an afternoon to go shopping, or see a child's play, or catch their softball championship game, let them go, armed with their mobile device and a laptop. Trust them to get their work done, and location becomes secondary.

The only constant in your employees' life is time. Let them use it to the best of their abilities, and not only will they rarely let you down, but more than likely, they'll work even harder for you.

LESSON: If you offer employees the option to work the way they want to when they need to, productivity will more than likely in-crease and corporate culture will improve, leading to happier em-ployees and thus happier customers. Added bonus: Employees will speak highly of the company in situations that could lead to better hiring opportunities for new workers—if happy employees can take time to do something important to them and not be penalized for it, they're going to share that with similar people—people who could also be beneficial to your company as employees.

TURN THE COMMUNICATIONS SPIGOT TO "OPEN" AND LET THE INFORMATION FLOW, FROM THE TOP DOWN

I remember when a good friend of mine found out she was being laid off from the advertising agency job she'd held for six years. Turns out the company lost a key account, and it was letting 200 people go worldwide.

First, my friend found out her company had lost the account. Then she found out it was going to have to downsize. Then finally she found out she was one of the people let go.

The problem was, employees found out all three of these things by reading an industry gossip website. At no point whatsoever, over the course of three days, did management bother to inform anyone in the company what was going on or make any kind of official internal statement. Instead, the rumors flew, employee trust went to zero, and it took several years after those people were escorted by security from the building for anyone to trust anyone else at that company.

That made for quite a difficult situation. As an added bonus, all of the agency's other clients heard the rumors, too, and were rightfully concerned. "Are you letting people on our account go? Should we be looking for other representation?"

It was a bad time and an amazing lesson in information management.

When you allow your employees to know what's going on as it's happening, you do several things. You shut down the rumor mill, you keep people focused on their jobs (because they're not gossiping about false information as much), and, most important, you keep a level of camaraderie and focused loyalty within the company.

LESSON: Have lines of communication drawn up that are usable whenever the need arises, and you're much more likely to keep your employees happy or, if not happy, at least not running for the hills. Once the storm blows over and the damage fades, you can get back to creating Zombie Loyalists, secure that you haven't lost any ground.

DON'T JUST HIRE EMPLOYEES; INVEST IN TALENT

A lawyer in Boston, Evan Fray-Witzer, started out as a journalist before switching careers. He told me about how he was treated as a rookie cub at a local newspaper, his first job out of college.

Way back when I was a reporter for a small McClatchy paper, they treated the young reporters (and editors for that matter) as investments. That meant they brought in advanced writing coaches and editors who sat down with us and went through our clips to talk about our writing and how to take it to the next level. It sent a very direct message that the paper was thinking of us as long-term investments. I've never worked for another publication like it.

That he remembers this fact from over 20 years ago tells you something—it's never a bad idea to treat employees as investments. It's been said before, it's cheaper to keep a current employee than train a new one. If you're constantly training new employees to replace old ones, not only are you wasting money, but you need to take a much deeper look inside your company. You don't have an employee problem, you have a *culture* problem.

LESSON: Employees are *investments*. Treat them with the respect they deserve, and help them grow.

FINALLY, TRUST, TRUST, AND TRUST (BUT VERIFY)

Ask any company what is the one thing that truly powers its corporate culture, and it will always, always come back to trust. Just as in a relationship, without trust, you have nothing.

If I can't trust my employees, what does that say about my business, about my hiring, about my ability to understand people?

If a company can't bring trust into its culture, nothing else will work. You'll never create Zombie Loyalists, because, well, what's the point? If the company doesn't trust the employees, and the employees don't trust the company, then how can customers trust either of them?

I'm not saying that any company should completely relax its guard and not double-check on occasion. But if a company doesn't have the ability to let the employees do what they were hired to do without constant worry, then the problem is much bigger than just trust.

LESSON: Trust your employees to do the right thing. Most want to, and when given a choice, most will. But employees need to be trusted, and companies need to extend that trust. Corporate culture is symbiotic.

IN THE END, having a fertile breeding ground for your zombies will almost always start with a great corporate culture. If you have that, you can pretty much do anything. The question is, though, do you have that?

Go through this chapter again and ask yourself how you stack up to each idea. What can you change? What can you bring to management to implement for a better workplace environment? How can you better motivate your employees to truly *love* what they do, where they work, and the differences they make?

Once you have the corporate culture in place to breed Zombie Loyalists, the actual breeding is the fun part.

So ... keep reading. Let's breed some Zombie Loyalist customers!

4

NOW THAT YOU'RE READY TO BREED, LET'S INFECT YOUR FIRST CUSTOMER

When you think about it, Zombie breeding is much more efficient than regular breeding. One bite, you're done. Much less messy than traditional breeding.

—Mentioned at a bar by a friend of the author's somewhere
between chapter one, two, and several drinks

It is a truth universally acknowledged that a zombie in possession of brains must be in want of more brains.

—Seth Grahame-Smith, *Pride and Prejudice and Zombies*

Chances are, the easiest way to grow your business may be to stop focusing on growing your business.

—Said anyone who ever had an "aha!" moment
as sales started going through the roof

ongrats! You made it to chapter 4. You took some time, implemented some new ideas to improve the culture of your company, and you're already light-years ahead of where you were before. You can actually *feel* the difference in the office every day.

Awesome. So your team is prepped, every employee knows that it's about the customer and is living, breathing, and eating that mantra. You're ready to start building an army! Now's the time to turn every single boring old customer into a Zombie Loyalist, ready to do your bidding and bring more and more Zombie Loyalists right to your door.

But it has to start with one. Let's create one awesome, truly devoted Zombie Loyalist customer in this chapter. Once we do that, making multiples will be a lot easier. After all, no scientist ever clones hundreds of sheep at once. That's dangerous. One molecule off, and you could wind up with a horrible, mutated, evil sheep army that would destroy our way of life.

This chapter presents a handful of stories from bona fide Zombie Loyalists. They patronize companies big and small in the United States and around the world. Their stories will show what you can do right now, today, to incubate your first Zombie Loyalist.

The key to successful breeding is to go in with the right frame of mind. I've said this before, but it needs constant repeating. In fact, it bears printing out and putting on your desk so it's the first thing you see every morning:

The general expectation of any given customer in any given service situation is that they'll be treated like crap and will leave neutral at best, unhappy at worst.

It's true. Think about your last few experiences with a fast food restaurant, an airline, a car dealer, or even traffic court. As I was writing this chapter, I asked 15 people on Facebook to rate their last experience from a customer service standpoint. I asked the question in the simplest way possible: Was it amazing, eh, or bad?

The results were pretty much in line with what was expected: 5 "bad," 8 "eh," and 2 "amazing."

I then followed up with each person and asked for more details. Let's look at one of the two "amazing" responses.

The first "amazing" response came from a woman named Andrea, who reported to me on her dinner at the same restaurant where she's eaten at least once a week for the past ten months.

Why did she rate it amazing? Well, they knew her, started making her drink the second she walked in, hugged her, cleared a table for her immediately, took care of her, made her and her dining companion feel like they were the most important people in the restaurant, and, essentially, treated them like family. (Treating customers like family is actually an essential skill that we'll talk about later in this chapter, because most companies that try it do it wrong.)

The key takeaway for Andrea's "amazing" experience is that she didn't have a "traditional customer" experience. Sure, she paid for her meal, but let's face it—she wasn't the average customer. If Andrea and her dinner companion arrived at the exact same time as two first-time diners, you'd see a world of difference between the two interactions.

What happened, sometime over the last year, was that Andrea ceased to be a "customer" and instead became a FOB—friend of the business.

"EXCUSE ME, SIR—ARE YOU A FOB? WELL THEN, RIGHT THIS WAY!"

FOBs have been around since the beginning of time. Homer Simpson is a FOB at Moe's Tavern; the entire cast of *Cheers* were FOBs at Cheers; and celebrities are FOBs at any business into which they walk. (Except Justin Bieber. It seems that more and more businesses are actively keeping him out.)

FOBs tend to be perpetual—that is, if I go to restaurant A a lot, or business center B, or even do my business banking with bank C a lot, I become a FOB. Once I'm a FOB, I like the way I'm treated, so I go back. I don't go to other places when I need something that I could get from the business where I'm a FOB, because I probably won't be treated as well as I am in restaurant A, business center B, or business bank C. In other words, familiarity breeds FOBs.

That's great. FOBs are great for business, because they come back a lot, they bring friends, and they tell the world about how much they love the business.

If I didn't know any better, I'd say that FOBs sound exactly like Zombie Loyalists.

I can actually hear you saying "That's awesome! We already have Zombie Loyalists, and we didn't have to do anything!"

Except that you don't, and here are two reasons why:

1. You *have* done something, but you haven't created a Zombie Loyalist. You've spent tons and tons of time on that one customer, priming him, marinating him, ensuring his FOB-ness. In Andrea's case, her local Italian place in Fort Lee, New Jersey, has been priming her to be a FOB for close to a year. That's a lot of work.

2. But a FOB is not a Zombie Loyalist. Zombies work in packs. Zombies attack in packs, and Zombie Loyalists come back to you time and time again because you treat them well—*but not just them*. And that's the *huge* difference between FOBs and Zombie Loyalists. If you take extra-special care of a FOB but treat all your other customers ordinarily, then you don't actually have Zombie Loyalists— you have 2 percent of your customers you treat better than 98 percent of your customers, whom you treat like crap, and that will come back to bite you.

Ever been stuck in the back of the entry line at a concert and get pushed out of the way by security as some guy you don't recognize gets escorted in? That's what it feels like to every customer (who rate you as "eh" when asked, by the way) as you step over them to cater to your three or four FOBs.

And that's a huge, huge problem.

FOBs are *not* Zombie Loyalists.

Now let's take a look at the "eh" category of my quick-and-dirty Facebook survey. The results were, more or less, what we expect from customer service today. The food order was okay (in one case, they didn't put the dressing on the side as requested), the oil change didn't take that much longer than they promised, the cable guy showed up near the middle of the eight-hour window rather than five minutes from the end.

It's expected, but that doesn't make it any less sad. It's still one hell of a commentary on how bad customer service has become. If a delivery of food or an oil change barely elicits an "eh," there's a lot of room for improvement.

But that, of course, is the good news. There's lots we can do to turn "eh" to "amazing" every time and for every customer—and it just takes a little bit of work.

The plus side to the "eh" crowd is this: They're actually the most accepting of change and the easiest group of people to convert into Zombie Loyalist customers.

Think about it: They're "okay" with what you gave them. They're not angry, they're not ripping you a new one on Twitter or anything. They weren't overly impressed, but they weren't mad. If this was high school and you were being graded on your delivery like it was a midterm, you'd get a solid C. (Maybe a C– if you forgot to put the dressing on the side.)

But you didn't fail, and you didn't lose a customer. That means they're ready to be infected. They're primed.

Finally, you have the five "bad" respondents. These include one person who was seen by his doctor more than 90 minutes after his scheduled appointment time, one coffee drinker who ordered one thing and got something completely different, and a person who's been unable to get hold of her bathroom contractor for the past four days.

Customers who have had "bad" interactions can also be turned around to become Zombie Loyalists, but it's going to take a lot more work. Recovering from a "bad" customer service interaction is possible and, when done right, can actually be very rewarding. Having turned problems into solutions for more than one client in various situations, I can tell you with complete certainty that there's no greater lover than a former hater.

But it ain't easy.

From this nonscientific survey, we can pretty much conclude that there are three potential outcomes to any customer service–based interaction at your business. The question is, which one is standard operating procedure, which one happens on occasion, and which one becomes the rarity?

That's up to you. Let's dig in.

For the purposes of creating our first Zombie Loyalist, let's focus on one respondent from the "eh" category, to show you what people usually expect.

Mark went in for his oil change at 11:30, having left work a few minutes earlier than his lunch break in case it took a little longer than the promised "15 minutes."

At 11:32, he pulled up in line. There were three stalls, each one with a car in the process of having its oil changed.

At 11:35, an employee walked over to Mark's car and greeted him.

Mark asked how long it would take, and the employee told him it wouldn't be longer than 15 minutes.

At 12:02, Mark was informed that his car was done. (The process took 27 minutes.)

Mark was in his car and driving away at 12:05.

I was writing this chapter on a plane, and when I asked the person next to me his thoughts on the 12-minute discrepancy, he told me it seemed perfectly normal.

If you didn't want to create Zombie Loyalist customers, I'd agree. Twelve minutes over the time promised really isn't that bad. Mark will probably return.

Right now, Mark is still just a customer. How do we get Mark to go from customer to Zombie Loyalist?

First, some background on the oil change place. It's not a chain. It's a local mechanic, which tells me that the majority of its customers are locals who either live or work right near there. (Small, independent businesses, take note here.)

Let's fix this.

SECONDS COUNT: BREEDING THE OIL CHANGE ZOMBIE LOYALIST

If I were consulting to that oil change shop, the first thing I'd teach management (not the employees, because remember, it has to come from the top down) is the concept of underpromising and overdelivering.

While it might sound good to say "15 minutes," in a day where everyone has a clock connected to every device, it's frustrating when it's not actually 15 minutes. And while some might not notice the delay because they're playing Words with Friends as they wait, the majority of people will certainly notice as an oil change starts eating into their lunch hour, and their internal thermometers will start to rise as you get closer to the 15-minute cutoff and go into the red as you go past the time promised.

So, if you're working in an industry where you're on the clock, can you set up the initial estimate to be one quarter longer than you know it'll take?

I asked Mark if he would have left if the employee had told him it would take 27 minutes versus the 15 he was promised. Not only would he not have left, but he would have walked next door and bought a sandwich, since he now knew he had the time.

Imagine Mark's delight when he came back 20 minutes later, and the car was done early and waiting for him.

Would this turn Mark into a Zombie Loyalist? Not right away, but you've probably guaranteed he'll return. In other words, you've infected him.

Now to prime the infection.

One of the biggest challenges to creating Zombie Loyalists is managing customer relationships. While there are tons and tons of software packages that can help, it's kind of a big undertaking, and one that small businesses might not yet be ready to dive into.

That's fine. As you grow, you can explore more expensive options. In the meantime, here's what I do with small companies to introduce them to the world of customer relationship management (CRM):

Start off by giving all employees 20 minutes per day where they're not changing oil but instead reaching out to the customers they've already worked with. Twenty minutes out of their day won't bring productivity down at all, I promise, and it'll actually increase Zombie Loyalist breeding.

Back to Mark: When he goes to the counter to pay for his oil change, he's already in a good mood, thanks to being able to get out of there earlier than expected. As he's being rung up, ask for Mark's email address. Explain to him that you're not going to spam him but rather you're going to shoot him a note when it's time to change his oil again, and you'll include a coupon not only for his next change but for his wife or a friend to do the same.

When the employee gets the email address, file it under Mark's contact information, thank him, and move onto the next customer.

At the end of each day, as the employee who worked with Mark is taking his 20 minutes to reach out, have him send one email to this address: 12weeks@followupthen.com

Follow Up Then is a simple, free service that does just what it says. The employee can add a subject line to the email with today's date and put all the names and emails collected today into the body of that email and hit send. It'll take less than a minute.

In exactly 12 weeks, that employee is going to get an email from Follow Up Then, with exactly what he put into it—the names and emails of everyone helped today. Then it's a simple task of writing this:

> Subject: Hey Mark: Time to change your Nissan's oil!
>
> Hey Mark: You came in about three months ago for an oil change. Just wanted to let you know that it's time to do it again.
>
> If you show me this email on your phone, I'm happy to drop 10% off the price of the oil change. In fact, bring in a friend with you, and I'll do the same for them.
>
> Thanks again for being our customer. If we can do anything else for you, feel free to reach out. You can get me at 212-OIL-CHANGE, and I work from Tuesday to Saturday, 8 a.m. to 7 p.m.
>
> Best,
> John

That's it. It's personalized, there's a valuable call to action there, and there's a built-in deadline (the knowledge that oil should be changed every three months).

When Mark gets that email, chances are, he'll return. And if Mark wants to look like a hero, he might forward it to his entire office, seeing if anyone wants to join him for the discounted oil change.

Remember: If Mark saves a friend money, he becomes a hero. This goes back to what we discussed in chapter 1: You get the customers you want by being awesome to the customers you have.

When Mark returns, he already knows his time to wait won't be long. He'll seek out John (because John has instituted a personal relationship with Mark, and John is the one who has offered the discount), and that will start a FOB relationship.

In this situation, however, a FOB relationship is perfectly okay, because the company is focusing on being amazing to *every customer,* not just to a select few. When Mark's friend meets John, that's another personal relationship, forged by a mutual friend.

The oil change location has just created two Zombie Loyalists, who now have:

- A personal connection with John, the guy who takes awesome care of their car
- A financial reason to come back
- A personal reason to come back (Time is valuable. They know John works fast and under deadline.)
- A FOB experience: "I bring my car to John, he knows me."

Finally, as we know, zombies have one goal: create more zombies. Mark will now do that, both with the coupon and with the recommendation alone.

Did you ever think it'd be possible to create a Zombie Loyalist for an oil change facility?

Fact is, you can create Zombie Loyalists for any customer at any store, business, or online site. All it takes is . . . wait for it . . . being one level above crap, which John obviously was today.

Does this sound simple? *It is!* I asked Mark what this scenario would do for him.

"I'd go back, no question. I was already going to, but when I got around to it. The email would probably bring me in earlier, and if I felt like I was going to get my car back ahead of schedule, I'd be more likely to go before the three months was up—I wouldn't have to worry about coming back to work late or anything."

What I found most interesting was what Mark said about the discount: "I'd certainly never turn down a discount, but for me, being able to bring someone with me and give *them* 10 percent off is a huge win for me. Who doesn't want to be a hero?"

Zombie Loyalists *love* to be heroes.

LESSON: Underpromise and overdeliver. If you do nothing else, that takes your customer service from "crap" to "wow!" Focus on nonintrusive, *beneficial*-to-the-customer follow-up (i.e., make them feel helped, not sold to) that's timed the right way, and you'll go from "wow" to zombie.

HAPPINESS AND PAYING ATTENTION:
BREEDING THE BODEGA ZOMBIE

Ever live in a big city? If you have, you know the beauty of the local bodega. Need a ham and cheese at 2 a.m.? Done. Coffee and an egg and cheese on a roll at 6:30 a.m.? No worries. Ex-Lax and a Diet Coke at 11:30 on a Tuesday night? Yup.

The thing is, though, there are tons of bodegas in any given city. You go to the one closest to your apartment, unless you're given a very good reason not to.

Enter Elizabeth Fullerton, a writer from San Francisco. There are six bodegas between her office and her apartment. Yet she only goes to one, two blocks in the opposite direction, and she visits it every single day. I'll let her tell you why:

> I wear headphones everywhere. I walked into this bodega one day, had my music on, wasn't even thinking about anything. The bodega counter guy asked what I was listening to. When I told him "TI," he sang, "You can have whatever you like" for a week every time I came in. We've started doing a little dance on either side of the counter as I walk up.
>
> When he noticed I stopped drinking, he started stocking more V-8 and lemonade without asking. If I'm in a hurry, he tells me not to bother with the coins. Do I go out of my way to patronize him rather than six other places on my way home? Oh yeah.

Think about this for a bit—this is a bodega employee who probably doesn't even think about creating Zombie Loyalists. But he's doing it anyway. Elizabeth is the perfect example of a Zombie Loyalist. She goes out of her way to give her money to a business, although many are much closer, easier to reach, and more convenient.

She does this every day. She tells people about this business, because she believes it to be a fun story. How often does your local deli employee dance with you when you walk into the store?

LESSONS FROM ELIZABETH'S FAVORITE BODEGA: Hire nice people. Hire happy people. Hire people who can get the job done, sure. But the person who just gets the job done isn't always the person who can best breed Zombie Loyalists.

PEOPLE OVER PROFIT MAKES MORE PROFIT:
BREEDING THE CAR DEALER ZOMBIE LOYALIST

Car dealerships have it rough. It's hard to work in an industry where everyone is suspicious of you to begin with. You'll never hear someone say in disgust "Ugh, he looks like a slimy chief of thoracic surgery," but everyone says "Ugh, he looks like a slimy used-car salesman." The car brand Isuzu even poked fun at itself that way in commercials in the late 1980s, featuring actor David Leisure as "Joe Isuzu," making obviously outrageous claims about its cars in an I'm-clearly-lying voice.

So when you can turn a car buyer into a Zombie Loyalist for your dealership, you've got some mad skills.

Melissa Schulz loves her Honda. She and her husband have had Hondas for years and find them to be safe, reliable cars. But loving a product isn't the same as loving the place where you bought it. (Example: I love my Samsung phone but can't stand the Verizon store.)

So when Melissa emailed me to tell me that she simply loves her car dealership, Buena Park Honda in Buena Park, California, I thought it worth investigation.

Melissa took her Honda to her dealership with a broken driver-side window. At the time, her husband was out of work, and this was an unexpected expense of over $500 that would have really strained Melissa and her family.

The manager of the repair shop was in the store at the time and quickly looked up Melissa's history with the dealership. He overheard Melissa talking to the salesperson and stepped in.

"Since you're such a good member of the Honda family, Melissa, we're going to fix your window at no charge."

Melissa, obviously, was over the moon. She actually went back to the dealership with a box of See's candies and a thank-you note. Did you get that? She went back to a place where she spent lots of money, with candy, to *thank them.*

What's the next car Melissa bought? Of course. And where did she buy it? Of course. And how many of her friends has she recommended to the dealership? Of course. And how many have bought cars from them? Of course.

I'd say the dealership bred one heck of a Zombie Loyalist with one move. In Melissa's words, "I will *never* forget what they did for me. Ever."

One small caveat, however: It was the manager who did this. If the manager hadn't been there, would the employee have been able to do it? Each company needs to make sure that each employee understands the value of going above and beyond in special circumstances. The best way to do this is to teach your employees what empowerment means and why you're empowering them to make their own decisions—to deviate from the playbook on occasion, as it were. Studies show that doing this actually leads to increased revenues over businesses that only allow runs by the book.

LESSONS FROM THE HONDA DEALERSHIP: If you take the opportunity to put people over profit due to special circumstances, the profit will almost always follow fivefold, and a Zombie Loyalist will almost certainly be born. The key is empowering employees to do this and trusting that they will use their powers wisely, not abuse them.

CARING COUNTS, AND SO DOES A GREAT PRODUCT: BREEDING THE LOCAL PUB ZOMBIE LOYALIST

The Red Stag, a pub in an old brewery in Halifax, Nova Scotia, is a place Carol Dobson finds herself quite often. Carol runs a public relations firm out of Halifax and started going to the pub several years ago.

She told me that she hadn't gone back in a few years but noticed that the pub was on Twitter, so she followed it. The owner of the pub, Adam Purcell, tweets under the name @theredstaghfx and is known for living by a philosophy of "caring counts." In Carol's words:

> Adam will tweet not as the bar, but as himself. He routinely tweets things like "I'm on my way to the restaurant, who wants a pack of Tim Horton's coffee delivered to a friend's office?" If someone responds, he'll grab a pack of coffee from the local Tim Horton's and drive it to the friend's office as a surprise, compliments of the person who responded and The Red Stag.
>
> He's also been known to mention that he's "accidentally" made an extra burger or two, after the lunch shift run has ended, for anyone who was too busy to go out and get lunch. He'll then have the lunch delivered, free of charge.

Obviously, he gets quite the reception in Halifax, and more often than not, his customers turn right into Zombie Loyalists.

Here's the kick, though: Anyone can drop off a cup of coffee. If the atmosphere at Adam's pub sucked and the food was horrible, all the burgers and coffee deliveries in the world wouldn't matter.

If your basic customer service sucks where it counts—that is, for the actual product—it doesn't matter what kind of fun and kooky things you do—you won't build Zombie Loyalists, and, worse, you might be considered a poseur.

Fortunately, the Red Stag in Halifax doesn't have that problem, because according to Carol, the food is excellent, the atmosphere is spectacular, and the beer is good.

That's a win, win, win, win!

Carol again: "I definitely bring him more business because of who he is and how he acts. I belong to a few organizations, and we're organizing dinner events. Guess where we're going?"

LESSONS FROM THE RED STAG IN HALIFAX, NOVA SCOTIA: Doing fun, off-the-wall things that are actually brimming with good deeds is a great way to promote yourself. But to make it stick, it can't just be "Hey, look at these crazy things we're doing." The Red Stag has a quality product, and once people come in, that's what hooks them. The better your product, the more successful your "caring counts" actions will be, and the more your Zombie Loyalists will drag new customers back, over and over again.

OBSERVING WORKS: BREEDING THE GREEK
RESTAURANT "BAD DAY" ZOMBIE LOYALIST

Ilana Jacqueline, a patient advocate in Boca Raton, Florida, had a really bad day. She and her fiancé went out to dinner at Greek Corner, a local restaurant they'd gone to once or twice before.

As they were digging into their meal, the owner, whom they'd never met before, came over, saying he noticed they looked like they'd both had bad days. He told them that no one was allowed to be sad in his restaurant so he was giving them a bad-day discount on their bill.

He returned a few minutes later with two shots of ouzo, then disappeared.

"We were floored by the free shots, and they totally helped," Ilana said. "We didn't expect anything else, so imagine our surprise when we got the bill, and there was a 10 percent off bad-day discount. Since then, we've gone back at least twice a month in the past year, and we've brought friends there both from in town and out of town. We love Greek Corner!"

The owner made Zombie Loyalists out of Ilana and her fiancé simply by *taking an interest*. He noticed that two people didn't look as happy as they could have. He didn't pry, he just said that he noticed and wanted to fix it. It wasn't creepy, it wasn't annoying, and free shots of alcohol are always a nice way to start a relationship.

LESSONS FROM THE GREEK CORNER IN BOCA RATON, FLORIDA: Observe and react accordingly. As you see problems with which you can help, step up. You never know where the next Zombie Loyalist will come from. In some cases, it's as simple as a "Hey, let's make your day better."

Quick Aesop's Fable break, because it's relevant: The story of Androcles and the lion.

A slave named Androcles once escaped from his master and fled to the forest. As he was wandering about there, he came upon a lion lying down moaning and groaning. At first he turned to flee, but finding that the lion did not pursue him, he turned back and went up to him. As he came near, the lion put out his paw, which was all swollen and bleeding. Androcles found that a huge thorn had got into it and was causing all the pain. He pulled out the thorn and bound up the paw of the lion, who was soon able to rise and lick the hand of Androcles like a dog. Then the lion took Androcles to his cave and every day used to bring him meat from which to live. But shortly afterward both Androcles and the lion were captured. The slave was sentenced to be thrown to the lion, after the latter had been kept without food for several days. The emperor and all his court came to see the spectacle, and Androcles was led out into the middle of the arena. Soon the lion was let loose from his den and rushed bounding and roaring toward his victim. But as soon as he came near to Androcles, he recognized his friend, and fawned upon him, and licked his hands like a friendly dog. The emperor, surprised at this, summoned Androcles, who told him the whole story. Whereupon the slave was pardoned and freed, and the lion was let loose to his native forest.

LESSON: Gratitude is the sign of noble souls.

Or, more specifically, if you can do a little something to cheer your customers up or make their day brighter, not only does it reaffirm in their mind the choice they made to patronize your establishment, but it also creates Zombie Loyalists, and a truly loyal zombie is as powerful a weapon as that lion in the fable.

YOU NEVER KNOW WHO'S WATCHING: BUILDING THE SUPERMARKET ZOMBIE LOYALIST

Lindsey Wolko of the Center for Pet Safety related a great story that had nothing to with her—except it has *everything* to do with her. She was shopping at Wegmans, a local supermarket chain, in Reston, Virginia. As she was shopping, she noticed an elderly woman, frustrated and confused, unable to find the product she was looking for.

She then watched an employee who was stocking the shelves—without being asked—put down his stock, walk over, introduce himself, and in a soft, soothing voice, tell the woman that he was going to be her personal store guide for everything she needed on that trip.

The employee walked the older woman around the store, getting her the items she needed. He then took her to the front and rang her up at a closed register, so she didn't have to wait in line. He packed up her items and made sure the woman was able to get home without incident.

Lindsey observed all of this. She has elderly parents that she cares for. That woman in the store could have been her mother or father. As Lindsey watched the care and concern this Wegmans employee showed the confused woman, she knew she was going to be, in her words, "a customer for life."

In our words? A Zombie Loyalist.

I should mention that when I put out my call for amazing customer service stories, I heard more about Wegmans than any other store or business, by a factor of at least 3. This tells me that Wegmans understands the entire process—from hiring, to training, to empowering its employees. You can't breed Zombie Loyalists if you don't have the right employees. Your employees can build you the largest army of Zombie Loyalists who will go out and bring you thousands of new customers each day, or they can destroy your brand and send your zombies across the street, never to return. If everything else is equal (product, quality, price), the tie-breaker will always, always be your people.

LESSON FROM WEGMANS FOOD MARKETS: It's nice to be nice for its own sake, no doubt. But you never know who's watching. And this applies to being *not* nice as well. All it takes is one customer to observe something negative—or, worse, capture it on a camera phone—and you've got yourself a little mess. But hire nice people—let your employees learn why nice is profitable, why nice matters, and why nice is just good karma—and you'll earn points not only from the people you're helping but from everyone in earshot as well.

HANDLING THE ANNOYING TASK SO THE CUSTOMER DOESN'T HAVE TO: BREEDING THE ELECTRONICS STORE ZOMBIE LOYALIST

Laura Stocker, out of Lemoyne, Pennsylvania, decided to splurge on a new radio for her car. Not a tremendously expensive purchase but not exactly an impulse buy either.

She dropped off her car at Creative Car Tunes to have the old radio taken out and the new one installed, and returned a little while later to pick it up.

Turning on the radio as she left, she noticed that the installer had taken the time to write down her previous radio station presets from her old radio and preset the same stations to the same numbers in the new radio. It probably took an extra minute, but Laura now has a little bit of delight and amazement to share from an otherwise normal transaction.

Laura makes a really good point: "Would I have been angry if they didn't do this? Of course not, but what a difference this tiny detail made as I pulled away!" And there's the key to turning a regular "eh" transaction into an amazing experience, worthy of breeding a Zombie Loyalist.

LESSONS FROM CREATIVE CAR TUNES: Those extra five seconds can earn you a lot of extra revenue, a lot of new customers, and, even if nothing else, some great brand loyalty and positive discussion. What kind of things can you do for your customers that they wouldn't think of expecting? Here are some of the most basic examples I could think of at 2 a.m. in Tokyo when I couldn't sleep:

- The Chinese restaurant that puts rubber bands around chopsticks when parents bring their children with them, so they can learn how to use chopsticks

- The women's clothing store that keeps a "husband couch" in the middle of the store, complete with a PlayStation and a TV tuned to whatever sports game is currently playing
- The waiter who brings over some extra blue cheese olives in a separate cup because he noticed how quickly you ate the first ones out of your vodka martini (and by "you" I mean "me")

It takes so little to create a Zombie Loyalist, and the opportunities for us to do so, each day, are simply endless. It all comes down to the level of creativity you have and the level of empowerment your employees are given.

YOU THINK THIS IS A GAME? WELL, IT KIND OF IS: BREEDING THE GAME STORE ZOMBIE LOYALIST

David Mayer plays *Magic: The Gathering.* Confession: I used to play it too. Anyhow, David did something that every young *Magic* player dreams of: He actually married a woman who decided that she wanted to learn how to play the game too.

David took his wife, Holly, to Ancient Wonders in Tualatin, Oregon. The second David and his wife walked in, the employees at Ancient Wonders sat her down, taught her to play, discovered her playing style, and got her hooked. They helped her grow her skills, suggested what types of cards and specific games to buy, and turned her into a fine match for her husband.

Once Holly and David were regular players, Holly convinced all her sisters-in-law to play as well, and of course, the entire family went to Ancient Wonders for the same experience. Now you have an entire extended family playing *Magic: The Gathering* and buying all their needs from Ancient Wonders.

This is a defining geek moment here, people. David told me that he's since moved out of Oregon but waits to buy new cards until he makes his twice-yearly trip back, so he can go to Ancient Wonders and stock up.

The staff at Ancient Wonders has learned how to use their geek powers for good, and they do it exceptionally well. Understand, I'm a huge fan of geeks. My first company was called the Geek Factory. So I'm beyond impressed. I might just have to visit Ancient Wonders the next time I'm out that way. And then I can bring home cards to my wife, who will look at them and just sort of shake her head in a sad I-guess-it's-too-late-to-back-out-now kind of way.

LESSONS FROM ANCIENT WONDERS: If you hire employees who are already madly passionate about what they do, make, and sell, empower them to take the time to go above and beyond, every day, by sharing that passion.

- Hire people passionate about what you do, and let them go to town on customers.
- Nothing beats passion. Not innate sales ability, not a smile, nothing.

The employees sat Holly down, seizing the opportunity to convert yet another person into the world of *Magic: The Gathering*. Once they succeeded, everyone won: The store won for breeding new Zombie Loyalists, Holly won for learning how to play the game, the extended family won by joining the fun, and, most important—I don't think any geek would argue this—David won by finding a wife who likes *Magic: The Gathering*.

WHEN AN EMAIL IS PERSONAL, IT'S NOT AN EMAIL, IT'S HELP. BREEDING THE MEMBERSHIP WEBSITE ZOMBIE LOYALIST

How many emails do we get a day from companies, businesses, and the like that we just delete without even reading?

MovingWorlds.org, a site that matches people with the best places around the world to volunteer their skills, fell victim to the same problem. People would request to join, and MovingWorlds would follow up but then fall off their radar.

Instead of an automated do-not-reply email that would, irritatingly, inform Megan Semjanovs that she forgot to finish her registration, she received an email from Mark Horoszowski, an actual employee at MovingWorlds.org. In this personal email, he simply dropped Megan a follow-up note and included his Skype phone number, a way to schedule a personal meeting with him, and made sure to tell Megan that he's also happy to answer questions about volunteering in general, not just about his company.

He closed with a PS, asking her about her unusual email address and the story behind it. This obviously wasn't a form letter.

Megan found this whole process different enough from the usual auto-responders we all get that she made sure to tell me about it—and also signed up and completed her registration with Moving-Worlds.org. As she put it, "It's a small gesture, but it really impressed me, and really went a long way."

LESSONS FROM MOVINGWORLDS.ORG: It has to be personal. No one wants to be emailed by a machine. People want interaction when they need it, especially if the task at hand has the potential to be annoying. What can you do to stand out and not be annoying? Some ideas:

- Allow each employee the opportunity to reply directly.
- Empower the employee to understand that a personal connection is light-years better than a corporate one.

When I worked for America Online back in the day, I occasionally helped in tech support, because I was a geek. I kept an alternate email address, and I gave it to every customer I helped. I told them that if they needed further assistance, just shoot me a note. More often than not, they shot a note of thanks and stayed in touch. Who doesn't want to have a friend in the business?

I know a little something about email and mailing lists. As I mentioned, I founded HARO, and at its height, I was sending over 1.2 million double opt-in emails per day. It was pretty amazing—especially because we had a daily open rate north of 70 percent.

Here's the kicker, though: Each email, every single day until I sold the company, came from my personal email address, peter@shankman.com. Not from a donotreply@wherever.com but from a real address—mine. That meant, when you had a problem, when you had a question, or if you just wanted to chat, all you had to do was hit "reply." I built Zombie Loyalists every time I sent out an email—because they were personal. They came from me. And if you wrote back? I responded, usually pretty fast.

Try it! peter@shankman.com. I'll wait.

IT'S NOT A MARATHON, IT'S A SPRINT. EXCEPT WHEN IT'S A MARATHON: BREEDING THE ENDURANCE ATHLETE ZOMBIE LOYALIST

Like me, Patrick Skittles Cooney is an endurance athlete. We both compete in triathlons, marathons, long-distance death-type races, and the like. Why? Probably because we both don't have much common sense.

A while back, Patrick told me about Skratch Labs, a company that makes all-natural hydration and nutrition products for endurance athletes. What started as a bunch of cycling dudes mixing up their hydration drink in hotel rooms during the Tour de France has turned into a booming business with some really fabulous products, several of which I use during long training rides and runs.

Anyhow, what I love about the company is that not only can you buy its stuff in many cycle and running shops around the world, but you can still shop for stuff on its website. In fact, right on the home page is the mission statement:

> Through our belief in real products, real ideas, and real people, our mission is to promote health and happiness—to be one of the best parts of people's day as they strive to be their best.
>
> If you're not completely happy with our products, or our service doesn't make you smile, let us know, we'll make it right.[1]

That tells you something right there. But here's what Patrick loves about the company: When you order products through the website, it also sends you samples of the products you *didn't* order, both as a thank-you and as an introduction. Skratch Labs includes the following card:

Photo by Patrick Skittles Cooney

You have to love a company that goes out of its way to thank you and give you more than you ordered, right?

Skratch knows that everyone loves freebies and makes sure to send some whenever you order. Do you come back? Of course. Do you buy more? Of course.

Do you tell the world? Of course.

Do you become a Zombie Loyalist for Skratch labs? Without a doubt. And I'll let you in on a little secret: There are some wicked-fast Zombie Loyalist cyclists out there. Sadly, I'm not one of them. I'm definitely a middle-of-the-pack racer. But that's cool too.

LESSONS FROM SKRATCH LABS: A thank-you is always a nice touch, and a thank-you with a freebie just goes above and beyond. Think about how many times you order from places online. Imagine how much more you'd love it if more companies did little things like that.

Then imagine how much more your company would be talked about if you did. It's not that hard—a few sample packets, the same kind you give away at trade shows and race expos. But now you're having a one-on-one interaction with someone who already loves your product—a warm lead, as it were. Everyone wins.

So . . . let's sum it up for this chapter—what have we learned?

- The majority of customer service interactions in the world fall into the category of "eh." It wasn't great, it didn't suck, I got my product, whatever.
- That leaves a ton of open room for being one level better than "eh."
- Start off simple:
  - A free tidbit added to an order
  - An extra bit of surprise and delight over Twitter
  - A few minutes of training on a new product for a newbie
  - Doing the extra little bit of work no one else wants to do
- Make the follow-ups about help, not about selling.
- Reach out using simple tools like followupthen.com when they work to your advantage, to get your feet wet in the CRM space.
- Let your products and the actions of your employees speak for themselves.

Last, understand this: You've just bred your first Zombie Loyalist customer, and you may already be enjoying the rewards that he or she is bringing you. But now, more than ever, you need to continue breeding. If you stop now, your one zombie will die. You need more.

Go get a cup of coffee or go for a run. Then come back, and we'll head into chapter 5, where we'll examine case studies that businesses are using to go from one or two Zombie Loyalists to a whole army.

Oh, hey—one more thing: Thanks for sticking with me so far. Is it useful? Let me know—tweet me @petershankman. I want to hear what you have to say.

5

AFTER PATIENT ZERO

HOW TO BUILD YOUR ZOMBIE LOYALIST ARMY

If you build an army of 100 lions and their leader is a dog, in any fight, the lions will die like a dog. But if you build an army of 100 dogs and their leader is a lion, all dogs will fight like a lion.

—Napoleon Bonaparte

Your Zombie Loyalist army has started to take its first steps toward global domination. Now is *not* the time to stop and rest. You've got momentum on your side. Now's the time to strengthen and grow your fighting forces! How? Through small moves that make a huge difference. Read on.

This is going to be a fun chapter for me to write and I hope for you to read as well. Why? Because I get to talk about companies big and small that totally and completely get it when it comes to building Zombie Loyalist armies, and they have the profits to prove it.

In other words, building armies of Zombie Loyalist customers to do your bidding is not only doable but easier than you think. Remember the Disney version of "The Sorcerer's Apprentice" in *Fantasia*? You know the part before the brooms took over the entire castle and got Mickey Mouse in a world of trouble? That middle part is what I'm talking about—zombies bring in more zombies, who bring in more zombies, and so on and so on. The stories here prove it. All you have to do is be a little bit awesome. It's not hard. If you've implemented the changes in culture we talked about a few chapters ago, if you focus on empowering your employees and giving them the freedom to make off-the-script decisions that can positively impact your brand, building your army will soon become second nature for your business.

HEADPHONES AND CORPORATE CULTURE: THE MAKING OF A BOSE ZOMBIE LOYALIST

If you've set foot on a plane even once in the past 15 years, you've seen Bose headphones. The company has always been famous for amazing audio products like speakers and radios, but over the past 15 years, it's also become known as the noise-cancelling headphones company, and it's got the stats to prove it. Next time you're on a plane, look around. Row after row of businesspeople wearing Bose headphones, listening to music, watching movies, or even just sleeping, thanks to the silence they afford.

But if you're a business traveler, you're also on the road a lot, and the chances of breaking them, cracking them, or leaving them somewhere rise dramatically.

Enter my friend and colleague Stuart Tracte. Stuart is not only a business traveler but a New York City resident who walks everywhere. As such, he keeps a pair of earbuds in his ears 24/7, like most people in major cities. When I asked him if he was a Zombie Loyalist for any brand, he sent me the following. I didn't ask him to. He doesn't work for Bose. He doesn't get paid by Bose. The simple fact that he took the time to do this shows you the impact that good customer service can have in building an army of Zombie Loyalists. Read what Stuart wrote, then we'll talk about it.

> Before there was Beats [the noise-cancelling headphone line designed by rap impresario Dr. Dre], there was Bose. Before it became cool to wear huge cans on your ears, Bose was making high-quality personal audio products and, for the most part, was alone in that category. A pair of Sony in-ear headphones, at the time the darling of consumer audio products, cost no more than $50, which was considered expensive for headphones. Along comes Bose with a pair of $150 earbuds. Why would anyone pay that much for a pair of headphones?
>
> I'll tell you why. I have gone through three pairs of their in-ear headphones over the course of about 12+ years. I had the first model. They were the best-sounding earbuds for a consumer price point that I had ever owned or experienced. When the cellphone market exploded, I needed a pair with a microphone to keep up with changing technology. These things

BLOW AWAY the stock Apple iPhone headphones. My third pair was to update to their newest model, a water-resistant pair of headphones that are more durable and can take the punishment of exercising with them on.

Product review over. What is the real reason I have been a Bose headphone customer for more than a decade? Customer service. Why do I rave and scream "BOSE" at the top of my lungs every time someone asks for a headphone recommendation? Customer service. Why will I be a Bose customer for life, and by default, a Zombie Loyalist? Customer service.

As a male residing in New York City, I'm faced with many challenges. Here's one: I don't want to carry a bag or backpack with me all the time. This makes it difficult to carry more than a wallet and keys. Forget about carrying a big pair of over-ear headphones. Where would I put them when not using them? Around my neck? Sorry, I'm not a DJ.

This is the plight of *many* urban men. Stuffing earbuds in your pocket. Untangling wires EVERY TIME you pull them out. This is not only abusive to our patience but also to a pair of headphones. Wires can degrade over time from always being bent and stretched. You might sit on your headphones and crush them. A litany of things can happen when you stuff headphones in your pocket.

Why go through all of this exposition? To prove the value of being a loyal Bose customer. Not a single one of these human behaviors prevents this company from standing by their product. I have brought Bose headphones back to their retail locations (they'll also do this by mail if you don't have a store in your area) and they will always honor their product and you as a customer. In fact (I'm not saying this is official policy), the first time I had an issue with my headphones (one ear stopped working), I had purchased them at Best Buy. I tried to return/exchange them for a new pair at Best Buy (I didn't have a receipt) and they denied my request. Say what you will, but $150 is a lot to spend on earbuds. I was disappointed that Best Buy didn't stand behind the merchandise they sold.

So, what did I do? I went to a Bose retail location in Manhattan (the Broadway location in SoHo) to try my luck. And it worked. They asked a few easy questions about when and where I purchased them. I was honest and said Best Buy. Without blinking an eye, the salesperson reached behind him and began unboxing a replacement. I was amazed and pleased. Not only did I get a replacement, but I got a new receipt and was now in Bose's system as a customer. I walked out of that store with a shiny new pair of headphones and the satisfaction that a company stood behind their product, regardless of where I purchased it.

On a few other occasions, I've had some issues with my headphones. Wires fray over time, I've stepped on an earbud and crushed it, the microphone stopped working, and a few other normal wear-and-tear problems. *Every single time,* I've walked back into this Bose store on Broadway and have been taken care of. No questions asked. I'm probably on my 6th or 7th pair over the course of 10 years, and I've *never even considered* doing business with anyone else. The peace of mind that comes with knowing that a company truly cares about the satisfaction of their customers and the quality of their products is more valuable than anything else. *Especially in a time when we, as consumers, feel like we're always getting the short end of the stick.*

I'll be a Bose customer for life. They give me peace of mind and confidence that they actually care about my satisfaction, not just my money. I'll scream from the rooftops how much of a pleasure it is being a Bose owner, and I've brought many of my friends over to the Bose world and watched as they become fans for life as well. When you have a great product and back it up with amazing service and support, it's easy to launch an army of Zombie Loyalist customers who will keep doing everything in their power to tell anyone who listens how great the product they love so much actually is.

While I'm grateful to Stuart for sharing his story, the true moral might be easily overlooked, yet it's radically important if you want an army of Zombie Loyalists to bring in new customers.

Bose makes great headphones. No one is going to deny that. But if Bose did nothing to help when they broke, cracked, got stepped on, left on a plane, dropped in the ocean, what have you, it wouldn't have an army.

The reason Stuart and almost every other customer will go to war for Bose is not just about the product. It's about the culture of the company. Read what Stuart wrote again: He bought the head-phones at Best Buy, and when he needed to return them, *Best Buy wouldn't take them back, but Bose did, without question, and without even being the store from which they were purchased!*

Stuart still has at least another 30 years of work and business travel ahead of him and then probably another 30 years after that of golfing, relaxing, and exploring. Just from Stuart alone, that's a minimum of 60 years of loyalty to Bose.

And let's talk about army building. Stuart is a friendly guy. He likes to chat with people. Much like me, he'll gladly talk to the person next to him on the plane, given the chance. He might share with them what he's watching (I know I carry a headphone splitter so the person next to me can listen to what I'm watching along with me) or, at the very least, share his music. When he does, he's going to talk about his headphones. His seatmate will listen and appreciate the quality of the sound, but then Stuart will start preaching from the church of Bose, and by the time that plane lands, chances are the person next to him has been converted.

Quality, and backing it up. That's how you breed an army. Walk onto any plane and look at what's sitting on the ears of almost any road warrior. You know beyond any shadow of a doubt—the Bose Zombie Loyalists have been here.

STEAK, PERSONALIZATION, AND ZOMBIES: MORTON'S THE STEAKHOUSE STORY

This story is one close to my heart, because it happened to me. I'm a bit of a steak lover. This will not be surprising if you've ever seen me. If you haven't, just Google a photo of me (your first reaction won't be "Wow, he must eat nothing but plants"). I try to eat as cleanly as possible, but I do have one weakness, and that's a good porterhouse.

When my alarm clock goes off at 3:30 in the morning, I know it's going to be a long day—because it means I'm going somewhere for a day and flying home in the evening. One-day round-trip flights are brutal, but I'd still take the occasional one-day round trip over never being able to travel any day of the week.

One particular morning I had to catch a 7 a.m. flight out of Newark, New Jersey, to Tampa, Florida, for a lunch meeting in Clearwater, then head back to Newark on a 5 p.m. flight. It was scheduled to get in around 8:10 p.m., so with any luck, I'd be back in my apartment by 9 or so.

I made my flight and got to my lunch meeting on time. Because of the training/workout schedule I was on (I'm always on some training or workout schedule), my first meal of the day was lunch, served during the meeting.

I had a healthy piece of grouper, and a very successful lunch meeting too, which lasted just about three hours. By the time I got back to the airport, it was close to 4 p.m. Boarding started at 4:30 p.m., so I didn't have time to stop for dinner and I didn't want to grab fast food at the airport, which would have totally defeated the healthy lunch. When I got on the plane, I was hungry.

Over the past few years, I've developed an affinity for Morton's restaurants, and if I'm doing business in a city that has one, I try to schedule a dinner there. I've become a "frequent diner," and Morton's knows it because of its spectacular customer relations management (CRM) system. It recognizes me—and my status as a "regular"—when I call from my mobile number. Remember how we talked about good CRM earlier? As you continue to breed your

Zombie Loyalist army, investing in a good CRM system is the equivalent of investing in good body armor: a necessity.

Back to my flight. As we were about to take off, I jokingly tweeted the following:

@petershankman
Peter Shankman

Hey @Mortons - can you meet me at newark airport with a porterhouse when I land in two hours? K, thanks. :)

I had absolutely no expectations of anything actually coming from that tweet. It was my version of a tweet like "Dear Winter, please stop, love Peter," or "Wish I was on a beach in Phuket right now!" I shut off my phone and we took off. Two and a half hours later, we landed at Newark. The fact that a flight got into Newark on time during summer thunderstorm season was a miracle in itself, a detail that will become important in a minute.

I walked off the plane and headed toward the area where the drivers wait, as my assistant, Meagan, had reserved a car to pick me up. I spotted a driver holding a handwritten sign that said "Shankman" on it, so I waved to him and started walking toward the door, expecting him to follow—a routine I've been through hundreds of times before.

"Um, Mr. Shankman," he said.

I turned around.

"There's a surprise for you here."

I turned to see that the driver was standing next to someone else whom I had assumed was another driver. Then I noticed that the someone else was in a tuxedo. And he was carrying a Morton's bag.

Now understand . . . I'm a born-and-raised New York City kid. It takes a lot to surprise me. *A lot.* I see celebrities on the subway. I see movies being shot outside my apartment, and fake gunfire from any given *CSI* or *Law & Order* taping, five days a week. I'm immune to surprises—except this one.

Alex, from Morton's Hackensack, walked up to me, introduced himself, and said, "We heard you were hungry, sir," and handed me a shopping bag that contained a 24-ounce porterhouse steak, an order of colossal shrimp, a side of potatoes, one of Morton's famous round loaves of bread, two napkins, and silverware.

I was floored.

I never, ever expected anything to come of my tweet other than some giggles and me-toos from followers.

Not only that, but Morton's Hackensack is 23.5 miles away from Newark Airport, according to Google Maps. That meant that in less than three hours, someone at Morton's Corporate saw my tweet, got authorization to coordinate the meal delivery, and then got the ball rolling by getting in touch with Morton's Hackensack to place the order.

Then Morton's Hackensack had to cook the order, box it, and arrange a server to *get in his car* and drive to Newark Airport (never an easy task, no matter *where* you're coming from or what time of day it is), then—and this is the part the continues to blow me away—while all this was happening, someone had to track down my flight, find out where I was landing, and make sure Alex would be there when I walked out!

Think about all the things that could have gone wrong: My flight could have been delayed or diverted. I could have exited from a different location. Had I taken the AirTrain and not had a driver, I would have taken an entirely different exit route! Of course, I could have just missed Alex all together. In fact, numerous other variables could have screwed things up. I have no doubt that countless companies have the same thought when a similar opportunity arises: "Oh, too many logistics. That'll never work," and they leave it at that. But what if it *does work?* What if it happens, and it works *perfectly,* and it shocks the living hell out of the person they do it to?

As it did that night?

And what if that person's first thought was to make it public? As I did? How long do you think it took me to share what happened, write a blog about it, and put it all over Facebook? About a nanosecond. We live in a world where everyone can be a broadcaster. Do you know *anyone* who *doesn't* have a camera in their phone, or anyone who *doesn't* have a Facebook or Twitter account? Customer service is no longer about telling people how great you are. It's about producing amazing moments in time and letting those moments become the focal point of how amazing you are, told not by you but by the customer you thrilled.

My tweet and subsequent blog about what happened was picked up by a lot of other restaurant, marketing, and business blogs. Roger Drake, senior vice president of marketing and communications at Morton's, explained that because the restaurant is active on social media and knew I was a frequent diner, when marketing manager Jillian Beard saw my tweet, she immediately reached out to Mike Khorosh, the general manager of Morton's Hackensack, to see not only whether such a delivery could be done but whether it could be packaged nicely. Mike thought he could pull it off with the help of staff member Alex Sariyan.

It's part of Morton's "random acts of kindness" philosophy, which it employs because it wants to make customers into "brand ambassadors" (otherwise known as Zombie Loyalists). Think about it—amazing experience? You'll share it, sure. But it's not just about one over-the-top stunt. Rather, at Morton's, it's part of a *culture* of service, and *this is the key takeaway.*

Morton's isn't in the business of delivering a steak to the airport for every guest, and it shouldn't be—that's not its job, that's not what it does well, and that's not financially viable by any stretch of the imagination.

But what Morton's does do *amazingly,* and what creates Zombie Loyalists each time, are small instances of "personalized wow" that cost almost nothing but deliver tremendous results. I'll explain.

Morton's isn't a cheap restaurant. It's not ridiculously expensive, but it's certainly not a "hey, let's go to Morton's for a quick bite" type of place. When you go to Morton's, you go to feast.

When you call and make a reservation, you are asked, *every single time,* if you're joining them to celebrate a special event or just coming in for dinner. Let's say it's your wife Wendy's birthday, and you're celebrating that at Morton's. When you arrive and are shown your table, the menu is in front of you, and guess what it says?

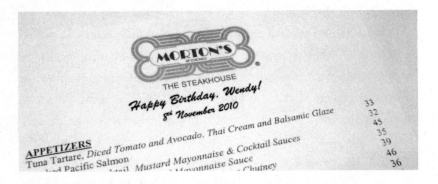

Crazy, huh? Go to Google and search "Morton's Menu Photos" and see what comes up. Anniversary wishes. Birthday wishes. Retirement congratulations, you name it.

Anyhow, Morton's does this for *everyone*. Not just VIPs, not just regulars, everyone. You show up at a Morton's, you're going to feel like a celebrity, you're going to be impressed, and you're going to share your story with the world. We're going to talk more about sharing in the next chapter. And the next time you're looking for a great steak, you're heading to Morton's. I've personally taken over 200 different people there and have thrown multiple events there. I have absolutely no financial relationship with Morton's, and the restaurant never pays me a penny for talking about it. I do it because, well, the service, plus, of course, the steak at the airport instantly turned me into a Zombie Loyalist. I, in turn, have gone and infected many, many others and will continue to do so as long as I have the ability to go to the gym the next morning and work it off.

DIAMONDS ARE A ZOMBIE LOYALIST'S BEST FRIEND: TWO STORIES FROM TIFFANY

The following two stories happened to the same company—one in 1980 and one just a few years ago. They have subsequently turned hundreds of people into Zombie Loyalists for Tiffany, the upscale jewelry chain.

In 1980, Meg Coldwells was newly engaged and working her first real 9-to-5 job at the General Foods headquarters in White Plains, New York. As she tells it, she was making a "whopping" $10,000 per year.

However, a lot of her friends and coworkers were getting engaged and married. (This was 1980, remember.) Meg decided to open up a charge account at Tiffany on Fifth Avenue in New York City so she'd be able to send quality gifts to these friends and colleagues. She filled out all of the paperwork and mailed it in. (For my younger readers, before the Internet, you had to mail things to places and then wait weeks for a response.)

A few weeks later, Meg received a form letter in the mail, denying her charge account. In her words:

> I was outraged! I was really pissed. I had had a checking account for years, was very responsible for a 21-year-old, had NEVER bounced a check and I was completely insulted. I decided to "take it to the top."
>
> I wrote a personal letter to Walter Hoving, chairman of Tiffany & Co., on my General Foods stationery, explaining the above and telling him I had been using my mother's account to buy things from Tiffany's for the last few years, but I was about to be married, had immaculate credit (for a 21-year-old . . .) and felt I deserved my own charge account at his store. I asked him to please reconsider my application.
>
> Within a week I received a personal letter back from Mr. Hoving that I still have to this day. It has 7 words. It reads:

"Dear Ms. Eigo, Will open. God bless," and was personally signed by Walter Hoving.

Think about that for a second, both what happened and the outcome.

- The chief executive officer wrote Meg back.
- She got her charge account.
- She kept the letter, showing it to everyone whenever the subject of customer service comes up, to this day, nearly 40 years later.

Does the CEO of a major company need to get involved in every customer issue? Of course not. But on occasion, when one does, a Zombie Loyalist is born (and remains one, nearly 40 years later.)

The key here isn't so much that the CEO wrote her back, although it does make for an excellent story. It's that, if you can teach

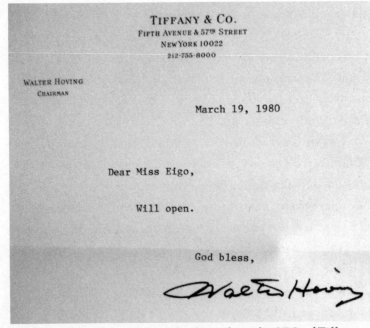

Meg wasn't lying; she did keep that letter from the CEO of Tiffany.

your employees that there is value in personally reviewing a situation when asked to, especially today, when everything is pretty much automated, you give them yet another way to create Zombie Loyalists.

How much money has Meg given Tiffany, has Meg's family given Tiffany, have the people Meg has told this story to given Tiffany? Hundreds of thousands of dollars, no doubt, if not more.

Here's where talking about Tiffany gets even more interesting: It's not just a CEO thing. Every employee is empowered to make those same types of decisions, as I learned from Brian Reich, who reached out to me on Twitter:

> My wife wanted a David Yurman ring as a gift. I couldn't find one and bought an expensive Tiffany ring instead. First kid born. Gift given. Wife not pleased. Lots of time passes, and I was too busy to return ring. Finally, went to do it and time allotted in ring return policy had long since passed. Scooped up baby and went to store. Asked for manager and started to plead my case (was supposed to be a gift, wife not happy, no time because of new baby) . . . Manager cuts me off. "Absolutely we will take it back, full refund . . . oh, and do you want me to validate your parking?"

As Brian told me, "Not only do I tell that story at every opportunity, but I have gone out of my way, including having Tiffany catalogs sent to people, to make sure friends, coworkers, and family shop there instead of some other jewelry store. I have no doubt Tiffany has made a ton of money from my referrals."

Brian is a Zombie Loyalist and breeds them for Tiffany because it took care of him when he screwed up. Meg does the same thing because it gave her a chance almost 40 years ago. The end result is that Tiffany generates a lot of revenue based on the culture ingrained in the company.

By the way, what have you done today that a customer will still have, in mint condition, 40 years from now?

You know what one of the best things about creating Zombie Loyalist armies for your company is?

Ninety-five percent of the time, all you have to do is simply open up an ear and listen, then react. The majority of your customers truly *want to like you, want to bring friends to you, and want to promote you.* Why? Because we're a society that *loves* being finders.

Finders are amazing. Finders are the ones people go to when they need to know what to eat, which new thing to buy, where to travel, and the like. Who doesn't love to give advice and know that it's appreciated?

Learn what it sounds like when finders have a question or want some answers, and be the one to give them what they need. That's how you build Zombie Loyalist army for your business, and that's how Maker's Mark bourbon does it too.

A KENTUCKIAN IN NEW YORK, AND A ZOMBIE LOYALIST IN THE MAKING . . .

Kevin Kuhn, born and raised in Kentucky, had just moved to New York City about 15 years ago. A little homesick, imagine his delight when he saw a billboard for Maker's Mark in SoHo, right near his apartment.

His friend, also a Kentucky native, made the effort to write to the company, explaining his connection to Kentucky and Maker's Mark and saying that he very much wanted to buy a copy of the poster, if it was available.

A month went by, and he didn't hear anything. Then out of the blue, his friend received a package with a framed copy of the ad, including a handwritten note wishing him well, plus an invitation to visit the distillery the next time he was in Kentucky.

To this day, Kevin regrets not having written to Maker's Mark himself as well. He made a copy of his friend's poster, but that's just not the same, is it?

Kevin closed his email to me with this comment: "Maker's Mark is not my favorite bourbon, but I still keep a bottle at home at all times, as a way to show my support for an extremely well-run company. I've told the story a few hundred times and bought more Maker's than I care to admit since then. Their $75 or $80 investment definitely paid off for them."

It's the little things. It's listening and making a customer happy. Do this over and over, and you have your army. In this case, it was a poster. That's it. Not the secret recipe for bourbon; just a poster, and the company has a Zombie Loyalist for life, who still buys their bourbon, even if he drinks another brand more regularly. What else could you possibly want?

Anyone want a drink?

A HURRICANE, A REPAIR, AND THE TRUE SPIRIT OF HELP: THE CREATION OF ZOMBIE LOYALISTS FOR RSC CONTRACTING

Joe Maida talks about most things with a calm, chilled-out tone. Except when it comes to RSC Contracting. Then, God help you if Joe thinks you're not listening to every single word he's saying.

When Hurricane Sandy hit Monmouth Beach, New Jersey, Joe's mother's house—the house where he grew up, the house that'd been in his family for three generations—took a massive hit. "There are a lot of memories in that house, and it means the world to my mom and our entire family," Joe said.

"My mom was evacuated during the storm and was devastated when the National Guard, two days later, allowed us back into the house to survey the damage. The entire first floor had to be gutted to the studs. Floors, walls, even some ceilings, all gone."

After Joe interviewed four different contractors, he chose RSC Consulting, or "the one that seemed to be the nicest," as he put it. He knew any of them could do the work and do it well, but he also knew it was going to take some time. Why not work with a company that's also nice, since you'll be seeing them every day for the next seven months?

Seven months later, Joe's mom's house was repaired and looked better than ever. Joe was blown away: "RSC Contracting did an amazing job, not only on the rebuilding/repairing of the house, but also in dealing with our insurance company time and time again to make sure we received a reasonable settlement to perform the work that needed to be done without cutting any corners."

You'd think that would be the end, right? It's probably enough right there for Joe to become a Zombie Loyalist, but RSC is about building an army of them. In Joe's words:

A few months after moving back into her house, my mom had a celebration and invited friends, family, and the contractor and all his employees who helped rebuild her house. When they arrived, they presented my mom with a beautiful photo album, the cover engraved with her name. The album was full of photos of her house before, during, and after the renovation that the contractor took as the work progressed. Rob Crotzer, the owner of RSC Contracting, didn't tell us he was doing it, but he was "secretly" documenting all the work during each phase of the rebuild by taking photos. Rob knew how much the house meant to our family, and he showed it with a wonderful gift for my mom.

Joe ended his story by telling me that he now considers RSC contractors not just a firm he hired but friends—and *no one* he knows does business with any other contractor, if Joe can help it.

LESSON: What can you do to stand out? Being nice is easy, but going the extra mile to be remembered, not simply recalled? Not only does Joe talk about RSC like they're family, but he brings out the photo album every chance he gets. Come on—the company took care of his mom and made her happy. What son wouldn't want to share that with the world?

When was the last time you posed for a photo with your contractor?

ICE WATER AND A PACK OF RUNNING ZOMBIE LOYALISTS FOR STARBUCKS

Sometimes it's hard for a large chain to do things differently. Unless the corporate culture specifically allows for it, employees actually can get into trouble for trying to help. (Remember my story about polishing the brass poles at the yogurt store?)

Occasionally, though, you do hear of great results coming from a big chain. In this case, a Starbucks in Raleigh, North Carolina, made a whole bunch of Zombie Loyalists out of Beverly Brown's running club, simply because they meet at Starbucks at 5:30 to go for their Thursday-morning runs.

As Beverly tells it: "The first time the baristas at my local Starbucks set out iced water for our runners' club, I posted a photo on Twitter and Facebook. On FB, I tagged all my runner friends. We still meet there to run at 5:30 a.m. Thursdays, and the baristas never fail to provide complimentary water."

LESSON: I'm pretty sure that Starbucks does a bit more business than normal on a Thursday, and probably other days of the week. The cost for new friends, new business, and a bunch of social media love? A few ice cubes.

TAKE ONE SPA, ADD ONE $15 COOKIE AND TWO ZOMBIE LOYALISTS, AND TURN THAT INTO $20,000 IN REVENUE

For some reason, Nancy Dibert and her husband decided to marry on Christmas Eve. Rather than celebrate their anniversary that night, they mark the occasion of their first date, a few days before Valentine's Day.

Wanting to do something fun for their anniversary, they discovered a new spa that had just opened, and I'll let Nancy tell you the rest.

In 2008, we lived in Maryland, where Envy Spa and Salon had just opened in January. We were looking for a nice place to enjoy a couple's massage and decided to give them a try. When making the appointment, the receptionist asked if it was for a special occasion or if Valentine's Day was coming early. I laughed and told her that we were celebrating the twenty-fifth anniversary of our first date, an annual tradition.

When we arrived at the spa, they met us at the door with a chocolate chip cookie cake iced with "Happy 1st Date Anniversary!" To say we were blown away is an understatement.

Due to the phenomenal first impression we had of the salon and staff, along with their continued commitment to customer satisfaction, we now frequent Envy Spa and Salon several times a month for our family's spa and salon needs.

Do they have better massages and salon services than any other spa? I'm not sure, but I'm not interested in finding out either. See, Envy went out of their way to forge a relationship with us, and I trust them and know that they will *always* go above and beyond. No matter how great the deal, I'll never be tempted by an offering from Groupon or Living Social. *Even with moving almost an hour away several years ago, we will still only go to Envy.*

The cost of that cookie? Probably around $15. The ROI? Thousands annually. Doing the math, with an average of $300 per month in salon services, we've spent over $20,000 with them in the past six years. When you count the friends that we have referred, that number is compounded.

The staff's kind and thoughtful gesture has made my husband and myself not only loyal customers but Zombie Loyalists to the utmost. It's the little things that count, and they absolutely nailed it.

A *cookie!* Are you hearing this? Not a private jet to take them to some magical Spa Island, but a cookie! We're a society that is so used to being treated like crap that something as simple as a cookie cake can cement over $20K in revenue!

Surprise and delight with the littlest things that show you care and that every customer is special, not just a number. What can you do, for the very next customer who walks through the door, to show that he or she matters?

ZOMBIE LOYALISTS OFTEN WEAR TUXEDOS: A STORY ABOUT VICTOR TALBOTS AND A CONFUSED MAN GETTING DRESSED IN 22 MINUTES

Several years ago I was in London for a wedding, and I'd forgotten to bring dress socks. I brought the entire suit and shoes, but no socks. Fortunately, I had a day to fix the problem, and London has more than enough sock stores to placate me.

Sometimes, though, it's not that simple, as publicist and event producer Harlan Friedman recalls. The takeaway here, though? The harder the problem to solve, the greater the Zombie Loyalism to whoever solves it.

In Harlan's words:

A Friday night in May is usually an easy night in the PR and marketing world. But this Friday, all the advertising and marketing agencies in Long Island were having their annual awards gala, and my business partner, Kerry, and I were invited.

I'm definitely a jeans and T-shirt kind of guy, but tonight I'd accepted that it would be an uncomfortable evening in my navy blue pinstripe, recently cleaned and pressed, in the car with all the accessories ready to go.

At 5 p.m., I look down at my phone and notice three missed calls from Kerry and as many text messages. That's never good.

Before I can call her back, the phone rings again, and she's screaming at me, something about "IT'S BLACK TIE! IT'S BLACK TIE!" The event started at exactly 6 p.m., one hour to go. Did I mention I was giving a speech?

My immediate response to her was that I was in a perfectly pressed suit and had no need to change. It was fine. Needless to say, that didn't go over well in the slightest, and by 5:05 p.m., I was on the phone calling tuxedo shops and men's stores within a 30-mile radius of me.

At 5:12 p.m., I call Victor Talbots. One of the last true "custom" shops, one wouldn't be out of place calling it a haberdashery. It's even known nationally for outfitting former football legend "Boomer" Esiason for his role on CBS's *NFL Today*. I call the shop at about 5:12 p.m. and ask what time does it close this evening. The gentleman who answers the phone explains that the store is about to close. I go into my frantic "I DON'T HAVE A TUXEDO AND NEED ONE IN LESS THAN AN HOUR" speech, and in response, I get a surprisingly calm "Come on over, we'll hold a tailor here."

While I was screaming down the Long Island Expressway at a speed that definitely should have gotten me pulled over, I figured I'd hedge my bets, and gave Men's Warehouse a call. As it turns out, it was open until 9 p.m. I let out a sigh of relief as I told them the story. Their response was a world of difference, however.

"Yeah, we're open until 9, and we have tailors on site here, but there's no way we can get you a tuxedo today. Sorry."

So much for that idea. At 5:34 p.m., I park the car (forgetting to close the door) and make my way into Victor Talbots. The next 22 minutes would be an absolute blur. I do recall tape measures flying, spinning around in dressing rooms, a small nip of Scotch, several laughs, and a few people throwing cuff links and suspenders at me.

Twenty-two minutes later, at 5:56 p.m., I was dressed to the nines, my street clothes packed up in a garment bag and a bottle of water in my hand, being helped back to my car— where, yes, the driver's door was still open—and on my way to the event.

What did Victor Talbots do out of the ordinary? They gave me assurance that the situation was sustainable and they would be there for me to assist. I can't begin to tell you how many people this story was told to, not even counting the 1,000 people I shared it with when it was my turn to speak at the evening's event. I took it to social media, where the great Boomer Esiason himself chimed in on the tweets, jokingly telling me to "never doubt him" when he endorses something.

I personally know several friends who have shopped there since and will continue to, and remember, they're not cheap. I've got to mention also that whenever I tell this story (and it's *often*), you can be sure that I also mention Men's Warehouse, and I'd be willing to bet that if I called them tomorrow, they'd go out of their way to get me in a tux now. But sadly for them, it's too late, as I'm a 100 percent Zombie Loyalist for Victor Talbots, and will be for life.

You know what I love most about Harlan's story? *We've all been in that situation:* I don't know one person who hasn't, at some point in their lives, found themselves without a suit, or a tux, or with a pair of jeans that had just split down the back when they bent over. (Not that that's ever happened to me . . . um. . . .)

I called Harlan after he sent me his story because I wanted to hear him tell it. You could *hear* the excitement in his voice when he got to the part about how the store put him in a tux. You could *feel* it when he said how he shared the story with over 1,000 of Long Island's top tastemakers and influencers that night alone.

Through the efforts of the employees at Victor Talbots, Harlan became not only a Zombie Loyalist but an invested member of the Victor Talbots community. He's the best kind of loyalist—the store got him out of a jam, and he's now a fierce protector of the brand for life. Introducing Harlan Friedman, the Victor Talbots' mastiff and Zombie Loyalist.

Never forget that someone in a crisis is already stressed. They're in trouble, and they need help. If you saw a car sinking in the river with a mother and child trapped inside, would you just ignore it and say it wasn't your problem? Of course not. The same applies here. Get someone out of a jam, and they become loyal. Go out of your way to get them out of a serious issue, and you've created the most loyal of the Zombie Loyalists.

At the end of the day, it simply comes down to this:

• People like to talk.

- People will talk about two things: great experiences and bad experiences.
- Whether you give them a great experience or a bad experience to talk about is 100 percent up to you.
- It takes so little to create a great experience that can bring you dividends for years, if not decades.
- If you empower your employees to do this, and they see the results, they'll keep doing it.
- Everyone will win: you, your employees, and your customers.
- The only ones who won't win: your competition.
- When all is said and done, this is supposed to be fun. If you're not having fun breeding your Zombie Loyalists, you're doing it wrong.

So . . . you're just about halfway done with the book. How you feeling? Got any ideas? As always, I want to hear them: peter@shankman.com or @petershankman on Twitter.

I'll close this chapter with a photo of my 11-month-old daughter exhibiting the exact same ADHD that I and almost every single one of your customers have. "Hey, let's eat some foo . . . Ooh! Shiny!"

Why did I put this photo here? Well, the first reason is obviously that she's incredibly cute. But there's a bigger picture here:

You have to assume that every customer who walks into your store, finds your website, orders from your menu, or hires you for a service has ADHD as well. And if people come in with short attention spans, it's not that hard for them to get distracted by something else.

That's why, during each and every interaction with customers, you simply *must* be better than normal. You must smile. You must interact. You must engage. You must listen. You must make customers so focused on you that they don't want to go anywhere else. They must know that they'll never find the same level of service, of caring, or of concern for their happiness that they'll find with you.

That's how you breed a Zombie Loyalist, whether they're businesspeople on deadlines, grandmothers of five, or 11-month-olds distracted by something shiny.

6

SPREADING THE WORD

SIMPLE WAYS TO ENABLE YOUR ZOMBIE LOYALIST ARMY TO TELL THE WORLD ABOUT YOUR BUSINESS

And they told two friends, and so on, and so on . . .

—Heather Locklear in a 1980s commercial
for Fabergé Organics Shampoo

I f zombies have one talent, it's that they're really, really good at making new zombies. They usually do this by walking around and biting people. While Zombie Loyalists don't bite people (which is good, especially from a legal standpoint), imagine how much more effective your loyalists would be for your business if you empowered them to tell the world how amazing you are using every form of social media and citizen journalism at their disposal. In this chapter, we're going to talk about how to do that.

There is no doubt whatsoever that I'm addicted to my phone. Fortunately, I take comfort in the fact that I'm far from alone in this addiction. I also take solace in the fact that at least I only have one phone for everything. My wife has two, and if one isn't ringing or buzzing, the other one is.

But being as connected as I am also means I share a lot. I mean, I share *a lot*.

I went through my phone just now and realized that I've shared no less than 20 "moments" in the past three days.

In random order, they included a photo of my feet on a plane, a steak from Morton's in Los Angeles, traffic on the 405, a group of 300 people watching me give a speech, a random man walking with a pet snake, a bunch of sandwiches from Jersey Mike's Sub Shop, and who knows what else.

Anyhow, the point is, I live on my phone, for good or for bad. For good are the photos of things that make me happy, make me smile, and, I hope, bring smiles and joy to my audience as well.

On the flip side, though, there was JFK Airport on Wednesday afternoon . . .

@petershankman
How the hell does Terminal 7 at JFK not have @TSA Precheck?

So as you see, sharing can go both ways.

Since we've spent the past few chapters talking about what to do to make sure your brand is positive, your message is clear, and your goal is to surprise and delight, let's turn our attention to how you can make it super easy for your audience to share for you, every way they can.

> **Golden Rule of Social Media for Businesses:**
> **A good number of your customers like to share moments in their life, whether good or bad. As the concept of sharing becomes more ingrained in our culture, that number will only grow.**

It's simply what we're doing, and each passing year gives us easier ways to do it, and more acceptance of it from a cultural standpoint. From people taking selfies after being pulled over, to photographing the finger they just found in their chili, people share. From posting their moods at any given moment, to creating memes on their mobile phones to express how they feel in real time, people share. When a moving airplane recently developed a smoke condition in the cabin, someone posted a photo of himself in the smoke before putting his oxygen mask on.

With every phone having a built-in camera (you can't buy a phone without a camera anymore; they're virtually nonexistent), with GoPro video cameras coming down in price while improving massively in quality (supposedly Felix Baumgartner, the man who "jumped from space" in 2012, did so with no fewer than 12 GoPro cameras attached to his jump suit), we're a culture that's quickly becoming addicted to sharing our lives, for good or for bad, in high definition, real time, as it happens.

If you add the growth of "wearable" technology, including Google Glass and the Narrative wearable camera, it's only a matter of time before everything that happens is captured in real time. The only question will be where it is shared and—if it involves your brand—whether the impact is positive or negative.

So, if everyone has the ability to share, and more and more people want to, it's up to you as a business to make sure you indulge your customers' wants in the most constructive way possible, for both you and them.

Remember, everything is more believable when it comes from a trusted source.

If you post a photo of your latest product on Instagram, with a caption exclaiming how amazing it is, potential customers find it much less believable than if someone in their network, whom they trust, posts the same photo.

We believe people with whom we interact, whom we consider friends, much more than we believe "brands." It's in our nature to be cynical, and social media has only compounded that cynicism.

Additionally, the chances of new potential customers seeing your posts are very limited, unless they're coming from people within their network with whom they've previously interacted. "Networks," whether they are Facebook, Google, or otherwise, are moving away from the follow-and-show method and more toward algorithms that show you content from what the network perceives to be your most valuable connections.

With that said, it's imperative that the majority of your shares come from *your customers* as opposed to from you directly.

How do you get your customers to share? (A tip: It's not by saying "Please share this!")

You get your customers to share by turning them into Zombie Loyalists who have reasons to share for you, and the number one way to do that is to provide them value that they believe makes them special. After all, we all like to be special. Let's explore 11 rules of spreading the word that businesses both big and small are using right now and how you can do the same.

The best part? You don't have to be a huge company to do this. The same surprise and delight that prompts someone to grab their smartphone and take a photo or update their status can be achieved by small flower shops just as easily as multimillion-dollar companies with huge social media departments. It's all about delighting the zombie.

RULE 1: ZOMBIE LOYALISTS SHARE, ON AVERAGE, TEN TIMES MORE THAN NON-ZOMBIE LOYALISTS

That's a huge stat with which to start this section, but it's true, based on some simple research within my Facebook and Instagram networks. Passionate customers of a brand tend to post much more about that brand over the course of their feeds.

It makes sense: If you already love a brand, you're going to share about it to begin with. But if the brand goes out of its way and does something extra special for you, you're going to go out of your way to share it. This isn't rocket science. This works for both business to business and business to consumer. There's no difference when it comes to loyalty; all that's different is how you share in each instance.

Let's look at Jennifer Roark Long. She was traveling with her two children and checked in to the Trump International Hotel in Chicago. Five minutes after arriving at her room, a knock on the door announced the arrival of a hotel employee with milk and cookies for her children. The kids were ecstatic, naturally, and Mom now had two very happy children.

Of course, she posted a photo to Facebook for all her friends to see.

But it brings up a bigger thought as well:

Who are Jennifer's friends primarily? In other words, who is in her feed? Who will see the photos she posts?

Well, I don't know Jennifer very well, but I'd venture a guess that a good number of people in her network are parents. Other moms, dads, people around her age, also with young children.

To quote Hannibal Lecter in *The Silence of the Lambs*, "We covet what we know."

And thanks to pretargeted advertising, search engines, and the Internet of Things, our networks also show us what we're coveting.

Example? The second I started researching online about having a child, my entire feed changed, within both Google and Facebook (the world's two primary sources of information). Not only did I start seeing advertisements related to my searches, but on Facebook, I started seeing photos, updates, and statuses from my friends who are also having, or already have, children.

The network understands us and anticipates our needs better than we do. (For an interesting article on this subject, look up "How Target Figured Out a Teen Girl Was Pregnant Before Her Father Did" in *Forbes*.)[1]

But back to Jennifer and her children at Trump International. As she was being amazed by the delivery of cookies and milk for her children, we also know who else saw the photo she posted: her friends and family, a good number of whom probably have children of similar ages.

If the need arises for them to book a hotel, where might they go? They'll remember Jennifer's experience.

Here's another interesting thought: They might not even have to remember it. As we'll discuss in later chapters, as the network continues to evolve and predict what we want, we won't have a need for sites like Yelp or Trip Advisor anymore. Instead, as we start searching for hotels, say, in the Chicago area, the network will simply show us the ones that we've already interacted with in some capacity—perhaps, in this case, when we liked Jennifer's photo many months ago.

The key takeaway here? At no point has Trump International had to advertise to you or ask you to "like" or "follow" it. Instead, the hotel and the best rates are being recommended to you based on a "like" you gave to Jennifer, several months ago, because an employee took the time to give her kids milk and cookies.

Customer service has truly become the new advertising, marketing, and public relations. Creating Zombie Loyalists are what will take you to the top of your category.

RULE 2: MORE OFTEN THAN NOT, THE LITTLE THINGS MATTER MORE TO ZOMBIE LOYALISTS THAN THE BIG THINGS

I'd say it's a pretty well-established fact that if you are running a company, you're doing so to make money. You might also contribute to the greater good, do wonderful things, and improve the environment, but if constantly generating and increasing revenue isn't the first thing on your plate every morning, there's a good chances you won't be in business for long.

This is one of the key reasons that the whole concept of "sharing" and "surprise and delight" so often take a backseat in marketing plans of small businesses. They can't envision any return on the investment; instead, they just think, "I'm giving stuff away for no reason, and it's going to cost me money that could be better spent on . . . anything else."

But what if it didn't cost a lot of money and, if you actually quantified it, it generated more revenue than, say, a traditional advertisement?

Enter Amy Nowacoski. Amy is the founder of a group called "Fat Girls Can Run," which, just as it sounds, is a group of runners who tackle everything from 5Ks to marathons. FGCR isn't Amy's full-time job but a labor of love that gets her, and countless women like her, out of their chairs and into running shoes every single day. It's a spectacular group of people.

Anyhow, Amy writes about running, blogs about running, talks about running. Along the way, she's mentioned that she likes LÄRABAR, an energy bar made from all-natural ingredients.

LÄRABAR noticed and sent Amy a package of products, including some new flavors that hadn't yet been released to the public, along with a note thanking her for liking them and being a customer. Of course, Amy posted a photo online and even wrote a blog post about it.

For the cost of six energy bars and minimal shipping, LÄRABAR took a fan and turned her into a Zombie Loyalist. According to Amy, it worked: "If I'm going to eat a bar, it would be LÄRABAR over anything else. Because LÄRABAR has treated me so well, I feel like a VIP with them. It's cultivated a sense of loyalty with me over any other bar."

Once every six months or so, LÄRABAR drops her a package of six or so bars. This keeps LÄRABAR top of mind not only in Amy's head but in her network as well. And how does this translate into

real revenue and a great return on investment for LÄRABAR? Well, Amy is a Zombie Loyalist to the brand. And those who are Zombie Loyalists to a brand, above anything else, have a mission to convert other people into Zombie Loyalists. Amy is no different. She explains: "There have been instances when I've been out at a supermarket, and I'll see someone standing at the 'wall of bars,' and I'll go over and make sure they know how amazing LÄRABARs are. There are a lot of people out there who eat them because of me."

Investment? Six bars per half year and minimal shipping. Return? Photos, blog posts, and multiple new customers.

RULE 3: THE BEST SHARERS ARE THE ONES WHO AREN'T ASKED FOR ANYTHING IN RETURN

Opportunities to create Zombie Loyalists who want to share for you are everywhere if you empower your employees to look for them.

Sometimes you can even turn the unborn into Zombie Loyalists, as a Red Robin restaurant found out last year.

The aptly named consumer website Consumerist relayed the story of a man who took his very pregnant wife and two-year-old son out for a dinner at the local Red Robin.[2]

The manager came over at one point and started talking to the family, asking if this was the woman's "last meal before heading to the hospital."

Upon receiving their bill, imagine the family's surprise to discover that the mother-to-be's meal had been comped, along with the words "MOM 2 BEE GOOD LUC" written as the discount item.

The photo of the receipt made its way to Reddit, a worldwide sharing website for anything cool, interesting, or newsworthy, and from there worked its way to ABC News, Consumerist, and a host of other news outlets and websites.

Consumerist reached out to this particular Red Robin, asking about the free meal. According to the interview, Charles, the manager, started out as a server and worked his way up. He clearly understands that the concept of what Red Robin calls an "unbridled act" is built in to the company's culture, and the company encourages this type of behavior.

"Treating our guests in a way that's special and unlike anything they'll experience at other restaurants helps us stand apart in a world where there are many options for dining out," he explains. "Our goal is to create lasting memories for the individuals and families who visit our restaurants."[3]

```
PIZZERIA PIZZA CHEESE           9.89
  BACON CHZ BG                  1.49
    SB RINGS                    5.18
  SODA (2 @2.59)
 MgrPromo                     -11.50
    Name: MOM 2 BEE  GOOD LUC
 Subtotal                      9.84
  Tax                          1.54

Total                         21.38
```

Much like Morton's and its menus, this is a small act with large, far-reaching consequences. Why wouldn't the recipient of this lovely act of kindness share it? Which she did.

You can't write a policy for each specific instance. As a company, you need to be able to say "Use your best judgment, and when you have the opportunity to delight a customer, do it."

The manager of the Red Robin decided that collecting $11.50 on a meal was less important than making a customer a Zombie Loyalist, and he was right. The return on investment here, thanks to the family being able to share their story, will last forever. (And no doubt they'll relay this story to their unborn child as he or she gets older, and the kid will have that same special connection.)

RULE 4: GIVING A CUSTOMER SOMETHING NO ONE ELSE HAS + MAKING SAID CUSTOMER FEEL GOOD ABOUT SELF = ZOMBIE LOYALIST WHO WILL SHARE

A great line from the series premiere of *Mad Men* came from Don Draper, when he was explaining to his client, Kodak, what the goal of advertising was:

> Advertising is based on one thing: happiness. And do you know what happiness is? Happiness is the smell of a new car. It's freedom from fear. It's a billboard on the side of a road that screams with reassurance that whatever you're doing is OK. You are OK.[4]

This has been true through the ages, but only recently has it been given an injection of steroids. Now it's not enough simply to be told that you're okay; you need a way to share with the world that someone else thinks you're okay too, a way to say "See? What I'm doing with myself is right; someone else thinks so too!"

If you work in any kind of retail business, you have the opportunity to tell your customers that they're doing okay every single time you make a sale.

The Twisted Root Burger Company in Richardson, Texas, takes this to heart by empowering employees to give out random discounts for whatever they deem appropriate to make a customer happy.

More often than not, they have fun with these discounts, and the end result is a sharable moment online.

As someone who's never gotten a "best butt" compliment in my life, I can tell you that if this happened to me, I'd share it far and wide and eat only at Twisted Root for the rest of my life.

I know I talk about empowering employees every other paragraph, but the fact is, it works. Great things can come from companies that have cultures of enjoyment, of making people happy, and cultures that say "We're in this because we enjoy what we do, and we believe that if we work to the best of our ability, we'll not only make a profit but have a great time doing it, and make other people happy as well."

At the end of the day, everyone wants to be recognized, whether it's employees or customers. If, as a business owner or manager, you can figure out ways to make that happen on a regular basis, your brand will grow, and you will create Zombie Loyalists.

RULE 5: A "THANK YOU" HAS A MUCH LONGER SHELF LIFE THAN A BRAG

If social media has turned our society into a bunch of oversharers, there are still some positives. One is the renaissance of manners. While people do complain a lot online (and we'll talk *all* about that in the next chapter), good manners have simultaneously made a comeback—especially the art of thanks.

Read any of the thousands of social media books floating around out there and you'll hear two words over and over again: "interaction" and "engagement." If you didn't know any better, you'd think these books were all telling you to stalk anyone who might possibly one day, if the stars align, buy your product.

To quote a popular meme, "Ain't nobody got time for that."

Rather, I encourage you to use the tools at your disposal to help encourage sharing from the customers you already have, who are just a few steps away from becoming Zombie Loyalists themselves.

I know of a very large casino in Las Vegas that has a "mentions wall" in its marketing department. Essentially, it's a giant screen, about four feet across by three feet high, that's constantly updating any mentions of the casino, on any platform, in social media. From this screen, teams of marketing bees can reply immediately to any compliments and jump on any problems, resolving them before they become too big to handle.

This is great if you're a giant casino with an unlimited marketing budget. It's not realistic when you're a small restaurant trying to survive.

But that doesn't mean you can't keep an eye out for "thank you" shares that you can use to your advantage.

@MissTRChatter
Had an **amazing meal** at Mohujos in Billingham last night. Excellent service too. Can't recommend it enough! I will definitely be going back!

Mohujos restaurant in Billingham in the United Kingdom has an awesome opportunity here to turn a fan into a Zombie Loyalist for life. All it would take is an employee empowered to reply, perhaps with something like "Thanks for coming in, @MissTRChatter—So glad to hear you had a great time. Let us know the next time you're coming back and we'll comp your party a drink!"

That's it! When she comes back, she'll be sure to let you know and probably will bring more people with her than she originally intended, since now she'll be the person who gets everyone a free drink.

If you have a customer relationship management (CRM) system, you can make a note with her contact details—"Thanked us via

Twitter, free beverage promised on next visit"—that will show up the next time she calls to make a reservation.

You're taking five seconds out of your day to make a customer feel just a little bit special. That's all. You're not wasting your time, you're performing a small act that will go a long way.

RULE 6: PROUD ZOMBIE LOYALISTS SHARE WITH HIGHER FREQUENCY THAN NON-PROUD ZOMBIE LOYALISTS

There are few sure things in life, but one of them, without a doubt, is that some of the best (or worst, depending on how you look at it) Zombie Loyalist sharers are either parents or pet owners. If you believe the rumor that the Internet is fueled by cats and baby photos, this statement will come as no surprise.

Lisa Marks is a designer in Brooklyn who, about four years ago, decided to see if she could toilet train her cat. I'll give you a second to digest that.

She'd purchased a new product called "CitiKitty," created by a woman in Pennsylvania. Lisa was happy to support a budding entrepreneur.

Sure enough, using CitiKitty, within a short amount of time, Lisa was able to train her cat to use the toilet instead of a litter box.

You can imagine Lisa's elation. Forget the pyramids, forget space travel—the pinnacle of existence for Lisa was teaching Cheeks to use the toilet.

Of course, she immediately took photos and, yes, even videos of her cat essentially doing what cats have been doing in the wild for millions of years but now on a toilet.

She sent the photos and video to CitiKitty, and a short time later, she received this reply:

Thanks for e-mailing CitiKitty your success story plus video and congratulations on toilet training your cat!

We are not sure if you are aware but we offer to ship a free CitiKitty to a friend or family member of customers that share their success story and photo with us like you have. If you would like to send a CitiKitty to a friend please let us know their address and we will ship it out.

If you have a moment, we would love to see your review of our product on Walmart.com and/or Amazon.com. Reviews like yours help cat owners decide if they want to toilet train their cat.

http://www.walmart.com/ip/CitiKitty-Cat-Toilet-Training-Kit/14997625

http://www.amazon.com/CitiKitty-Cat-Toilet-Training-Kit/dp /B000F1OS20

We will post Cheeks's video on CitiKitty's Facebook page soon. Be sure to check it out!

Congratulations again. We look forward to your reply!

Kind Regards,

CitiKitty Inc.

Amazing Cat Products!

Of course, this gave Lisa a new cause in life, as a Zombie Loyalist for CitiKitty.

Not only did she post reviews everywhere humanly possible, but when CitiKitty did in fact post her photos and videos to its Facebook page, she shared them far and wide. That one free CitiKitty unit it would send to one of Lisa's friends was an infinitesimally small price to pay for the number of people who would, after being influenced by Lisa, train their cats to use the toilet.

Postscript: CitiKitty has since been featured on the TV program *Shark Tank* and has grown by leaps and bounds, primarily due to the love and ambassadorship of CitiKitty fans and Zombie Loyalists.

It doesn't matter what the product is—if it's good and if people have a great experience, the chances are high that they'll share it.

Oh, and because you know it just has to be shown, please meet Cheeks, Lisa Marks's toilet-trained cat.

Over and over again, these examples prove that it's the little things that matter the most. What can you do, today, right now, to create Zombie Loyalists and encourage them to share?

There's a restaurant in Seattle that tracks the terms "landed" and "SEA" (Seattle's airport) in its Twitter searches. It simply has a computer at the hostess stand, and when she has a second in between seating customers, she looks to see if anyone has tweeted those two words in the same tweet.

If she finds a tweet containing both words, she quickly enters the Twitter name into the restaurant's CRM system to see if the person has ever eaten there. Depending on the result, she sends out a quick tweet either inviting the person to check out the restaurant and have a free drink or inviting the person to come back and have one.

Best case? The restaurant gets a new customer or a returning one, and the process of creating zombies starts anew. Worst case? The restaurant has welcomed a weary traveler to Seattle in a show of city spirit. It's a no-lose and takes a few seconds only. An added bonus, however, is that when those travelers *do* see those tweets, whether they drop by or not, replies are common, starting a conversation that perhaps will result in a new customer if not this trip, then perhaps next.

RULE 7: ZOMBIE LOYALISTS AREN'T
LIMITED TO SERVICE INDUSTRIES

One of the biggest complaints I hear a lot about the concept of creating Zombie Loyalists who share is that it doesn't work in non-service industries. In fact, nothing can be further from the truth.

Sure, service-sector businesses tend to get more shares as a whole, because they're offering tangible products, such as a pizza or a hotel stay. But if you look at almost any non-service industry business today, you'll see that the ability to tell your story and create Zombie Loyalists is just as powerful.

DPR Construction is a great example. It's a construction company with many high-profile corporate contracts, so you wouldn't think it would be ripe for creating Zombie Loyalists who like to share.

But DPR is smart. It doesn't simply post what it's doing; it *shares*. That's a huge difference. DPR works to make sure that the things it's sharing are actually worth sharing as well as reposting. Simply put, DPR works to *humanize* construction. Judging by the interaction it is creating, DPR seems to be doing a great job.

RULE 8: ZOMBIE LOYALISTS ARE PARTIAL
TO NICE, HUMANISTIC COMPANIES OVER
CORPORATE WORKER DRONES EVERY TIME

A friend of mine works in office supply, handling the maintenance, sales, and service of office equipment: copiers, printers, scanners, and the like. We met several years ago when I spent a few months as an in-house consultant at a big company, and he was there at least twice a week. We stayed in touch, and I try to recommend him to clients whenever I can.

Anyhow, for April Fool's Day this year, he'd heard of a prank that had been floating around the Internet for a while and decided to have some fun with his clients.

During each one of his sales calls on April 1, he made sure to attach the following sign to every printer:

You can guess what happened next. He would wait for someone to use the printer and shoot a few seconds of video. Then he uploaded the videos to YouTube (with the clients' permission, of course). He wound up getting links back from some high-profile websites, where people loved his sense of humor.

Is that how to create Zombie Loyalists for your business? Well, it's certainly a start. Several clients asked for the video to show their family and friends and to post on their own social channels. My friend was happy to send it—complete with a watermark on the bottom of the video, linking to his company.

New clients? Possibly. But increased exposure and recommendations for him from current clients? No doubt. That's how you breed Zombie Loyalists in the business-to-business world, and it's not really that different from the consumer world.

RULE 9: ZOMBIE LOYALISTS ARE FIERCELY LOYAL AND WILL SHOWCASE ANYTHING THAT HAS YOUR LOGO ON IT—ANYTHING

Back when I was running HARO, I learned early on that the best way to breed Zombie Loyalists, apart from personal interaction, was to constantly thank them when they used what I'd built. As such, I spent a good deal of money on HARO shirts, hats, sweatshirts, stickers, and the like.

We gave them out when people posted on our wall, when people tweeted at us, or when people had a good experience with the product. We encouraged users to send us photos in our shirts and highlighted the best and wildest places we found our logo.

By being generous with our shirts, hats, and the like, we created Zombie Loyalists who looked at our swag as prizes, not as our self-promotion. We were everywhere, and we were happy to spend the money to make more and more stuff to give away for free. The exposure was spectacular. People would send us photos of themselves wearing a HARO shirt next to the pyramids of Egypt or while running races around the world, and we gladly featured them and showed off our most loyal zombies.

What can you do to encourage your zombies to share? What tools do you have? What can you create?

RULE 10: ENCOURAGE ZOMBIES TO SHARE, AND THEY'LL FOLLOW EACH OTHER TO DO IT

In any zombie movie, when the hero is trying to avoid being eaten, he'll sneak around very quietly. Usually he'll run into a whole group of zombies who haven't noticed him yet. He'll stay very quiet, because he knows that if just one zombie sees him, all the zombies will head in his direction, and he's history.

Zombie Loyalists share the same hive mentality as real zombies. If a few start doing something, the rest usually follow along.

This isn't a bad thing, unless you're losing your zombies, and we'll talk about that soon. But when it's positive, it's a great thing.

Look at Kum & Go, a chain of convenience stores in the Midwest. Known for being irreverent and quirky, its actions are the same online as well as off. It has a large social media following and fiercely loyal customers.

*Really want to impress me? Show me your logo
on a NASA astronaut's helmet.*

"My boyfriend took me to @kumandgo for a shake, that's how I know he's the one" was a recent tweet that a store retweeted, and there's no doubt in anyone's mind that it wasn't sarcasm but a shout-out from a Zombie Loyalist who truly loves the brand.

That's why when people started tweeting photos of their Kum & Go coffee cups and food orders online, the store started retweeting them and sharing the photos online.

It quickly became a challenge. Could I post my coffee cup and get it retweeted? The answer was almost always yes, because Kum & Go loves its fans and knows that Zombie Loyalists will go out of their way to share. And when they do, they deserve appreciation. That's how you keep a good zombie happy. Well, that and the occasional hot cup of coffee.

RULE 11: ZOMBIE LOYALISTS BREED
FASTER THROUGH EXCLUSIVITY

If you've ever heard of the American Express Black Card, you know that it's the stuff of legend, a card with an unlimited credit line, made of titanium, that affords instant access to clubs, restaurants, and events most people can only dream about. People have written letters to the president of American Express promising to pay the hefty yearly fee and never even use the card, if they can just have it to show it off. In some circles, it's truly the symbol of having made it.

Very, very few people ever receive an American Express Black Card, and that adds to the mystery. Those who do have it are secretive about it, and those who don't want in.

Seeing this, another consumer-facing brand decided to do the same thing. Imagine Carla Caccavale Reynolds's surprise when she opened her mailbox one day to find a black credit card. But it wasn't from American Express; rather, it was a loyalty card from Dunkin' Donuts, with $50 on it, for one of, as Dunkin' put it, its "very best guests."

Now, let's face it. Reloadable cards are nothing new. You can buy one from almost any store for any amount of money.

Except when you can't. The Dunkin' Donuts Black Card isn't available at any Dunkin' Donuts store. You can't order it online. You need to be "chosen" to receive it. And when you are and you get it, believe me, you tell the world.

Carla says she definitely buys more people coffee then she ever did before, and of course, she only buys it from Dunkin'. "I know this isn't an ostentatious card, but rather, something fun that Dunkin' sent me to thank me for my loyalty, that very few people have. And that's what makes it fun to show to people."

How best to do that than to use it to buy coffee for someone at a Dunkin' Donuts? Zombie Loyalist acquisition: complete.

THE EXAMPLES IN THIS CHAPTER are just a small showcase of how to let your zombies share for you. Each company is different, with different corporate cultures and customers. Some are much more buttoned up than others, while some companies just have fun with their zombies.

But at the end of the day, Zombie Loyalists are humans first and foremost, and human beings have a need and a desire to share both good and bad experiences with their networks. In many ways, sharing validates us, allowing us to tell the world what's happening and the impact it's having on us, for better or for worse. When those impacts are positive, Zombie Loyalists are created, and giving them ways to share leads to positive attention for your corporate brand. And as I have said before, when someone people trust shows positive attention to your brand, the payoff for your business can be huge.

Your Zombie Loyalists are already carrying on them the tools to recruit and infect other Zombie Loyalists. All you need to do is give them the reason to do it.

7

YOU LOST A ZOMBIE!

HOW TO REGAIN YOUR LOST ZOMBIE LOYALIST BEFORE HE TURNS ON YOU AND DESTROYS YOUR BUSINESS

This is the part in the movie where that guy says, "Zombies? What zombies?" just before they eat his brains. I don't want to be that guy.

—Holly Black, *Kin*

This is CODE RED! There's nothing more dangerous to a business than a Zombie Loyalist scorned. It doesn't matter how it happened; what matters is what you do *next*. A scorned Zombie Loyalist has the power to take all of his or her infected zombies somewhere else. You can't let that happen; the effects could be devastating. You need to get your scorned zombie back into your good graces. Here's how.

SO . . . YOU'RE HAVING A FINE DAY UNTIL . . .

So you've spent all this time, huh? You've worked so hard to change the corporate culture. You've implemented policies. You've cut loose the deadweight. You've focused on the happy and the exciting while coming up with new ways to create, breed, and infect Zombie Loyalists. You've seen what happens when they get behind you, and you've experienced the thrill of your zombies forming an army in your name.

But then something happens. One of your zombies has a problem. All of a sudden, one of your loyal zombies starts to turn on you. He starts to ask what he's fighting for. He wonders if he really does have the best of everything with you. He starts asking himself if his loyalty is misplaced. He might even start looking around to see if anyone else wants him. After all, he's a perfectly good zombie, more than willing to help build other zombies for the right company, and he's shown his skills and dedication for several years. Perhaps he starts reaching out and seeing if his talents would be better suited elsewhere.

You're about to lose everything you've worked for.

ANOTHER AIRLINE STORY

Back in 2004 or so, I was already a Zombie Loyalist to Continental Airlines. I'd been flying it for about five years or so and thought I was a pretty frequent flier. (Turns out I wasn't even close, relative to how much I travel now.)

Anyhow, I decided to finally use some of my miles and do a quick weekend trip to London. I figured I'd buy a coach ticket and use my miles to upgrade to first class, where I could enjoy a flat seat, extra legroom, and somewhat decent food.

Imagine my shock when I punched the dates and location of my trip into Continental's website and found that to use my miles to upgrade, I'd be subject to a $500 fee *each way*. So much for the "free" in "frequent," huh?

Something to keep in mind about this story—Twitter and Facebook weren't around. I had no "followers" or "fans," I was just a guy who flew Continental Airlines a lot and was floored at being hit with these kinds of fees, considering how loyal I believed myself to be.

"This is how they treat their best travelers?" I thought to myself. This won't stand!

I did some digging and found the email address of Larry Kellner, the president of Continental Airlines at the time. I fired off a relatively professional yet definitely pissed off email—I think I used the term "nickel-and-dimed" and possibly mentioned something about exploring Delta or American Airlines as a replacement.

I sent the email, feeling slightly better but doubting I'd get any satisfaction. A few hours later I walked back into my office after a meeting, to find the voicemail light blinking. I hit play:

"Mr. Shankman? This is Larry Kellner with Continental Airlines. I got your email and was wondering if you had a minute to chat. Give me a call at . . ."

I wish to this day that I'd kept a recording of that message. I must have played it back 15 times to confirm it was real. Finally I called the number. A woman answered with "Larry Kellner's office."

"Um, hi," I stammered. "This is Peter Shankman, I think I missed a call fr—"

"Oh yes, Mr. Shankman," she cut me off. "Please hold for Mr. Kellner."

Click, click. "Hi, Mr. Shankman? Larry Kellner here. How are you?"

To be honest? Floored is how I was.

"Hi, Mr. Kellner. Um . . . how are you?" was all my shocked brain could make my mouth say to the president of one of the largest airlines in the world.

We then proceeded to have a lovely conversation that couldn't have taken more than two minutes. He explained to me that Continental had added several new super-low coach fare options for US-UK trips, and, because they were so cheap, they weren't eligible for mileage upgrades. He mentioned the email that was sent to all Continental frequent fliers (which to be honest, I probably looked at and threw away in an ADHD moment).

He then told me that he was going to wave the round-trip upgrade fees for me this time, to thank me for my loyalty. With that, he transferred me back to his assistant, who put me right in touch with ticketing, and two minutes later, I had a first-class round-trip ticket to London for the price of a cheap coach seat.

Again, I was nothing more than a 75,000-mile-per-year flier at the time. There was no social media, my blog had probably eight readers, and I'd published no books. I was simply a customer who was loyal to my favorite airline and was now pissed off. Continental noticed that and took action.

Fast forward to 2014: I'm still completely loyal to Continental (now United) Airlines. My business travel gives United hundreds of thousands of dollars in revenue each year. (I'm writing this chapter from a plane on the way back from Los Angeles.) I'm a huge fan of the airline and go out of my way to try to convert people. My relationship with United is definitely one of Zombie Loyalism, and when my daughter was born, United sent me a pink onesie with the United logo and the words "Oh, the places I'll go" on it. You know darn well a photo of her in it was on my Facebook page in about three seconds.

Back in 2004, Larry Kellner found out that one of his zombies was about to leave him, and he took immediate action to reinfect me. He did a heck of a job. Ten years later, I'm still with United, and I would rather connect through three cities on it than take a flight on another airline. Not bad for two minutes on the phone.

Remember, screwing up is easy to do. It's what you do next that determines your fate.

What follows are lessons from which I hope you learn. They contain both corporate and consumer wins and losses.

What I want you to take away from this chapter is this: You're reading all of these lessons long after they happened. You'll be sitting there and saying "Well, duh, the customer had been with them for ten years, I can't believe they didn't bend the rules for her," and think that no business could ever be that stupid, right?

Hindsight is 20/20. In the heat of the moment, could you guarantee that your business would say or do the right thing, every single time, to keep a customer happy or, more important, keep a Zombie Loyalist from defecting?

Before you dismiss some of these stories, think about the bigger picture: What if it happened to you? And not five years after the fact but in real time? Are your employees empowered to make the right decisions to keep a customer spending with you for years down the line, even if it costs you a few bucks in revenue now?

I once knew a boss who made sure every employee knew the first rule of his business: No employee would ever be let go for spending money to keep a customer happy but would almost certainly be fired for letting a customer leave unhappy, without doing everything in his or her power to try to fix the problem.

ZOMBIE LOYALIST SAVED: HOW PATAGONIA TURNED A LOYAL CUSTOMER INTO A ZOMBIE LOYALIST FOR LIFE

Farnoosh Brock runs Prolific Living, a company designed to help you get happy. Pretty awesome gig if you can get it, huh?

Farnoosh had purchased a piece of luggage from Patagonia and used it religiously for ten years. Right around that ten-year mark, the luggage ripped. (If you ask her, it simply "ripped." If you ask her husband, she stuffed way too much into it.) But either way, Farnoosh wanted it fixed.

Knowing the warranty was up, she called Patagonia and told her story. Expecting a typical "Sorry, it's out of warranty" response, Farnoosh was shocked when Patagonia offered to fix it for free; all she had to do was send it to the company. Which she did.

Her loyalty was tested, though, when, two years later, she used the bag for only the second time since the fix, and it ripped again. This time, she was hesitant to complain about a 12-year-old piece of luggage with no warranty, but she remembered the great experience she had the first time. She called and the customer service person told her to send it in and they'd see what they could do, but no promises. If the company couldn't fix the bag, it would send her a gift card.

That's where most companies would throw in the towel, and Zombie Farnoosh would head over to another company. Instead, Patagonia told her that no, it couldn't be fixed but thanked her for her loyalty with a nonexpiring $160 gift card, to use on anything Patagonia sells. All this for a piece of luggage over 12 years old and definitely out of warranty.

Needless to say, Farnoosh is a Zombie Loyalist for life with Patagonia and tells her story whenever she can. Hopefully, she now packs a bit more lightly too.

ZOMBIE LOYALIST LOST: THE JAWBONE FIASCO

This is the story of how a two-dollar cable cost a company a lot more in lost revenue.

Steve Hultquist is a textbook early adopter. As a technology journalist, he knows what's going on in tech long before the masses. He focuses on using tech as a tool to help get stuff done faster, better, and more productively, instead of buying the latest toy because it's shiny and new.

I'll let Steve take it from here:

When the first Jawbone came out, I was looking forward to it. The idea of a noise-cancelling Bluetooth headset was very promising for me, given that I was often on the road and also needed to be on the phone. Making sure that the person on the other end could hear me well regardless of my environment was a promise I looked forward to having fulfilled.

My first Jawbone performed well, and I was quite pleased. When the company announced the Jawbone 2, I was once again on their preorder list, looking forward to having a smaller headset with even better audio characteristics. My friends were often subject to my comments about the Jawbone, and a number purchased them on my recommendation.

I ran into an issue with the Jawbone 2, however, and arranged for a return. My assistant packaged the headset in its original box with all accessories and sent it in for repair. What came back was a working headset but nothing else. No box, no charger, no instruction booklet, just a headset wrapped in bubble wrap.

My assistant called Jawbone support and was told that their RMA [return merchandise authorization] instructions specified that only the headset was to be sent in, and nothing else. As a result, the company did not have the other materials to return to me. My assistant was devastated. She came to me with grave concern, knowing that I relied on the headset every day and feeling that she had made a terrible mistake, and offered to pay for a charger. I told her it wasn't a problem, and I was sure that Jawbone would help us out and send us a charger, at least. I didn't really need the rest of the packaging. So, she called them back.

And, shockingly, they didn't budge. At all. Just, effectively, "No, you're out of luck."

I will say that she also let them know that I had a bit of influence on social media and that I was a technology journalist as well. You would think they might be swayed. But they weren't—not at all. They simply said "No."

YOU LOST A ZOMBIE!

At this point, I was incredulous. They must not understand! So I called myself. I got the same answer. I let them know how this seemed to me, especially since I was sure the charger couldn't cost them more than a couple of dollars. They stood their ground. I was out the charger, but they'd be happy to let me buy a new one.

So I did, and it was the last thing I will ever buy from them.

I felt violated. My loyalty and enthusiasm was trampled by the very company I had praised. They had made it clear to me that their processes were more important than a happy customer, that their reputation was worthless to them, and that they couldn't care less about me or my pleasure in using their products.

Not long after that, I purchased my first BlueAnt noise-cancelling headset. I have bought a number of BlueAnt headsets since then, including the voice-activated Q3 that I now use, and recommend BlueAnt to everyone who asks.

I am still shocked that a company like Jawbone would not see fit to make a customer happy at relatively low cost. As a result of this mistreatment, I will never buy a Jawbone product again, and I will encourage others to seek alternatives as well.

Ouch. I mean, just . . . ouch. Note that Steve was told no multiple times, by different people, proving that it's part of the culture at Jawbone, not just one rogue employee.

Something also worth noting—BlueAnt is now plus one zombie, and the company didn't even have to work for Steve's love—as long as its product worked and it didn't include a note in the packaging saying how much it hated him, the company probably couldn't lose Steve if it tried.

Think about it this way: If you find yourself stuck with a broken-down car on a lonely highway in the pouring rain and cold wind, and a tow truck comes along to help you, do you wait because a better tow truck might come a little while later? No! You jump in that tow truck and dry off!

That's why losing a Zombie Loyalist is so dangerous. When Steve left Jawbone, not only was he angry; he was insulted. He'd personally put his reputation on the line for a company that had now shown its true colors. Assuming the company would eventually act the same way to someone Steve recommended, he would look bad.

As long as BlueAnt doesn't completely screw up, Steve will probably be with the company for years and years and spend quite a bit of money with it as well. All because of a two-dollar charger.

ZOMBIE LOYALIST LOST: THE ONLY THING WORSE THAN A PROMISE NOT FULFILLED IS A PROMISE NOT FULFILLED THREE TIMES IN A ROW

Melinda Masse relays a story out of Texas that simply didn't have to be, and that's what makes it all the more frustrating. There's nothing worse than giving a company more than one chance and having the company blow it every time.

This lesson is a simple one: If you're given a chance to keep a Zombie Loyalist after a screwup, consider it a gift, and act accordingly. Remember the saying "Fool me once, shame on you, fool me twice, shame on me"? What customer wants to feel foolish? Melinda certainly didn't:

There is a relatively popular Italian restaurant near my home. Great food. Great service. I went in at least once if not two or three times a week for takeout. I'd order my meal, have a glass of wine at the bar while I waited, and then eat the dinner at home.

One day I decided to get dessert too. Right before they brought me dinner, the manager came and asked if I wanted a different dessert. When I said no, he told me they didn't have what I wanted but would "make it up to me next time." Okay, it happens, right?

The next time I went in I specifically asked if they had the dessert before I ordered it. They said yes. Then when they were about to bring me my meal, the manager asked me the same question: Would I rather have a different dessert?

When I said no, he told me that they didn't have what I wanted. So not only is he not making it up to me, but, in fact, I was lied to when I called an hour earlier and was told they had my dessert.

This time the manager replied with "I'm sorry. My supplier f*cked me. I'll make it up to you next time."

I gave them one more shot, and you guessed it, the same thing.

I let the manager know that there would be no next time, and he had the nerve to respond to me with "Of course there'll be a next time!"

I haven't been back since, and you know what the worst part is? I would have been happy if he'd just said "I'm sorry" and then given me either a modest discount or not charged me for the cheap glass of wine I'd been drinking. But they never wanted to do anything in the present; it was always "next time."

Whenever someone asks for a restaurant recommendation now, I make sure to tell them where *not* to go, and whenever someone suggests going there, I tell them why we'll be going somewhere else.

Of all the ways a business can keep a Zombie Loyalist who's threatening to leave, "I'll make it up to you next time" is probably the least effective.

There is no next time. By next time, that zombie is being wooed by another restaurant, just down the street.

The restaurant manager committed the cardinal sin of Zombie Loyalist care: He let an unhappy zombie leave without a clear plan to make her happy again. He could have comped the wine, he could have discounted the meal, anything. Instead, he released an unhappy Zombie Loyalist back into the wild, where she could easily be captured and infected by another restaurant, which is exactly what happened.

ZOMBIE LOYALIST LOST: WHEN A COMPANY GETS ACQUIRED, THERE CAN BE DISSENTION IN THE RANKS. WITHOUT BEING CAREFUL, YOU'LL LOSE

Lots of things happen when a company gets acquired. Processes change, things that were once standard are no longer, and, more often than not, the company that's led the acquisition has to find quick ways to boost revenue to cover the debt of the sale. That's usually to the detriment of the longtime customer, aka the Zombie Loyalist.

Such was the case when Jeannie Wainwright's longtime local business bank was acquired by a much larger regional bank. It didn't take Jeannie long to start to see cuts in service and special services replaced by charges and fees.

Disappointed, Jeannie called and asked how to start the process of closing her business account. Shockingly, the customer service person she spoke with suggested that she call the branch where she opened her account.

Say what?!

When someone calls you and says "I'd like to take all my business away from you," the *last* thing you do is tell them how to do it! You *at least* ask why. Offer an apology. Anything!

But no. Jeannie was simply told to go to the branch where she opened her account.

So she did, and on a rainy winter's day, she walked into her old bank and started to close down the account. Shockingly (or not so shockingly), the branch manager was very interested in changing her mind and did everything to get Jeannie to stay, but to no avail. This zombie had already been infected by another bank, and nothing her old bank did could keep her from fleeing.

As Jeannie put it in an email: "Really, who takes a phone call inquiring about how to close an account and doesn't ask why? No way they were going to win me back. And I refer everyone to my new bank."

Is there anything worse than being given all the warning signs that you're about to lose a Zombie Loyalist and doing nothing in your power to try and save him or her?

How's my zombie? Still zombie-ing? Good. Anything we can do to make you more zombie-like?

There's nothing worse than being blindsided by a Zombie Loyalist loss that you absolutely, positively didn't see coming.

To lose a Zombie Loyalist despite your best efforts is one thing, but when one simply up and leaves, and you don't know about it until the zombie's gone, that's the worst.

If you're head down and working, sometimes it's easy to miss when a client or customer is unhappy, especially if no one tells you. In a perfect world, you could reach out to every customer once a month and just say hi. You could check in, get feedback, ask about the kids, and so on. But in the day-to-day effort of running your business, especially if you're a small business, it's not that easy.

With that, I recommend that my clients figure out a way to check with their top ten Zombie Loyalists and a random sampling of ten "regular customers" once a quarter. Whether it's a personalized email sent to each one individually, or a quick chat by their table when they come in for dinner, or even a check-in when you stop to refill their water coolers, there's no better way to avoid the blindsiding loss of a zombie than by knowing what's going on with him or her in real time.

That's what kept Michael from bailing on a local private bus line that ran from his neighborhood outside of Los Angeles into downtown LA.

ZOMBIE LOYALIST SAVED: HOW A LOCAL COMMUTER BUS KEPT A ZOMBIE FROM GETTING INTO HIS CAR AND DRIVING OFF WITH SOME DECENT REVENUE

"I'd been riding the same bus to and from work four days a week for about six years," Michael said. "I live well outside the city, and

I'm one of those strange Californians who prefer public transit to driving. Although the trip is long, it's convenient, and I can get work done both ways instead of sitting in traffic."

Over the course of several months in 2011, though, Michael noticed a decline in service. Initially, the bus was late, first by a few minutes, sometimes by as much as a half hour. Twice it didn't arrive at all.

Michael had asked the driver about the decline in service but never received a satisfactory answer.

One day in late 2011, Michael recognized the district manager on the bus. Michael sat down next to the man and introduced himself as a longtime rider who was getting a little fed up and was considering going back to his car.

The manager listened and, more important, took notes and promised to get back to Michael in the next two days. Sure enough, two mornings later, the bus pulled up to Michael's stop on time, with a brand-new driver. The district manager stepped out to welcome Michael back onto the bus.

A little bit of investigating on the district manager's part showed that the driver was completely disregarding several standard operating procedures. As such, the driver was taken off the route and sent back for retraining. A senior driver was put in his place, and the manager made sure Michael knew all of this.

The manager also gave Michael his personal mobile phone number, with clear instructions that if the bus was ever more than five minutes late, to call him personally, and he'd pick him up himself and drive him to work.

Three years later, and Michael is still with his bus service, four days a week. The bus service retained not only Michael as a customer, but who knows how many other people on that route?

Today, part of the standard operating procedure for that bus company is to have district managers ride every line at least once a month, introducing themselves to riders and offering several ways to be contacted if they have any questions or comments.

Ridership is up, customers are happy, and if you look down the 405 on any given weekday, you'll see a bunch of smiling, productive Zombie Loyalists on their way to work.

Business books always talk about "eating your own dog food." Make sure you're using your products, make sure you try them out to find the mistakes. Solid advice. But eating one can of dog food a quarter when your customers eat eight cans a week isn't going to reveal much to you.

In Michael's case, his bus had been having problems for months, but no one in any management capacity had noticed them. Had Michael not happened to catch the district manager that day, he probably wouldn't be a customer anymore.

Companies need to listen, both online and in person, as well as be there and check to see what's happening before the zombies tell them about it. And if you miss something and you find out from the zombies, jump into action, lest you wake up zombieless.

ZOMBIE LOYALIST LOST: KISSING THREE GENERATIONS OF ZOMBIE LOYALISTS GOOD-BYE BECAUSE YOU WON'T FIX YOUR MISTAKE

Imagine having a banking relationship that spans three generations. It starts with stock given to you by your grandmother and ends when a company won't fix its own error.

Enter Sun Trust Bank. Peggy Jo Shaw had been with Sun Trust since it was Crestar in the early 1980s. Unfortunately, at some point in the past year, a computer upgrade caused Peggy's account to go from the kind that had no fees to a new kind—one with lots and lots of fees.

The software had "grandfathered" the old type of account, so that the people who still had it could keep it, but no one could get it if they didn't have it. Of course, Peggy did have it; it was the bank's error that caused her to lose it.

She spent days talking to the bank and even wrote a letter to the CEO in Virginia. She never got any type of response, and of course, the customer service people kept telling her that the kind of account she wanted wasn't available anymore.

You can imagine how frustrated Peggy was. As she told me, she felt "betrayed."

One computer error caused a third-generation customer to feel betrayed and move not only her account but her children's college funds, her savings, and even her mortgage away from Sun Trust.

Anytime a customer mentions the word "generations," it's usually a good idea to listen. If you're a third-generation customer, you're a Zombie Loyalist from way back, and it really takes a lot to make you walk. Unfortunately, on occasion, the policies put into place by companies to generate more money actually wind up costing a lot more, as evidenced by Peggy taking three generations of zombies (and who knows how many future generations) across the street.

Again: Each case is different. Giving employees the leeway to make decisions for themselves usually will keep zombies from fleeing—especially if they've given you ample warning that they're about to leave.

ZOMBIE LOYALIST LOST: JUST BECAUSE YOU'RE THE KING OF YOUR LAND DOESN'T MEAN YOU CAN'T EASILY LOSE A ZOMBIE

Diapers.com is one of those great, incredibly simple sites that just works. Need diapers? Order them, and they arrive. Duh. Prices are competitive, and the convenience is something to talk about.

That's why when first-time moms try diapers.com, they're usually hooked. The ease of use keeps them coming back, and as long as everything works as it should, all is well.

There's a downside, though, even if it's not readily apparent: When everything works really well, it's the easiest thing in the world to create Zombie Loyalists. In fact, it's the very way that Amazon launched itself into the consciousness of every customer in America and then the world. Buy online, it ships, and it arrives at your door. Rinse, repeat. Zombie Loyalists abound!

But when something stops working as it should, you need to take action immediately. There's no more scorned Zombie Loyalist than one who expects greatness, because that's what you've given in the past, and receives mediocre service at best and full-on mistakes at worst.

So it should come as no surprise that Ioana, a mom from Chicago, was in love with diapers.com from the moment she tried the company in 2009. As it grew and acquired more sites, such as soap. com, she was easily spending $400 to $500 a month with it.

But over time, Ioana says, things stopped being perfect, which was surprising to her.

> The bigger the company got, the more problems I had with them. Most of the time the way they packaged the products I ordered was faulty, so almost each time something spilled or got damaged, and I had to spend time cleaning stuff and calling to report the problem.
>
> I explained to them multiple times exactly what went wrong (too many products stuffed into boxes way too big) and gave them suggestions on how to improve their packaging. Although they credited me every time I called and replaced the damaged products, in the end, they lost my business. My time is too important to spend it on the phone with their customer service.

The worst part is that Ioana asked to speak to a manager before she left diapers.com completely, hoping someone would work with her to keep her. Nobody ever bothered to reach out.

As Ioana says, "The problem is not that they lost my business, but they are also losing money by being so inefficient and having to award credit back to unhappy customers and pay way too many customer service agents to deal with them. I doubt I was one of their biggest customers, but I am sure that 6k worth of orders every year is not to be let go so easily."

Four months later, Ioana is happy with Amazon's subscription service that sends her what she needs, when she needs it.

One of the most dangerous things about having a company that breeds Zombie Loyalists so quickly is that when things go wrong, you can lose them just as quickly, if you don't pay attention.

The great thing about cultivating Zombie Loyalists is that they're usually willing to work with you and give you multiple chances to get it right. As the stories in this chapter suggest, if, even *after* those chances, you're still screwing up and, worse, don't see any need to change your practices, don't be surprised when your zombies make a beeline to a competitor and take them your brand and your revenues with them.

ZOMBIE LOYALIST SAVED—ALONG WITH CLOSE TO $2,000 IN REVENUE

Welcome to Newton Highlands, just outside of Boston, and a small restaurant called O'Hara's. This is where, every Saturday night, we find Dennis Napier, as he grabs takeout for himself and his wife.

There was no greater Zombie Loyalist for O'Hara's than Dennis. Over time, he got to know the wait staff, and it really became "his" place. Recommendations flourished, and he often sent friends there.

After a while, however, he started noticing errors. Minor things, but enough to give him pause. He mentioned it to the manager, but they kept happening. Finally, after several "last times," his order was screwed up yet again, and Dennis was done. He let one of the wait staff know that he'd written the restaurant off after giving it too many attempts to get things right.

About three months later, he received a text from the bartender asking for a final shot—saying there'd been "changes," and Dennis needed to see for himself.

Skeptically, Dennis went for one final try at Saturday-night takeout. In his words:

When I got there, the owner ran over to me, shook my hand and said "Thank you for coming back and letting us prove to you we value you as a customer." My takeout order was packed to perfection, and he refused to let me pay. When I protested, he told me I had done them a favor because I helped them identify a weak link in their process for getting takeout orders processed and out the door correctly. What I truly appreciated, however, was that they accepted responsibility, developed a plan to win me back, and have been spot-on ever since.

According to Dennis, that was well over a year ago, and at $40 or so per Saturday-night dinner, per week, that's not chump change for a small restaurant. More important, Dennis is back to telling the world about O'Hara's and shares his love of the restaurant with anyone who will listen. This zombie was recovered.

Here's the thing: You're going to screw up. It happens to everyone. As we said before, though, the key is what you do next.

In Melinda's case earlier in the chapter, the restaurant had a chance to fix her problem and keep its zombie, but it chose not to, incorrectly assuming that she'd just be back and accept it. In Dennis's case, management stepped in, fixed the problem, apologized, and proved itself. Two similar stories, with two completely different outcomes.

Losing one zombie might not seem like a big deal: "Oh, it was only one customer." And you're right, it was only one. But if you look at it from a medical perspective, it's an entirely different story:

If you wake up one morning and find yourself with one pimple, you're probably not going to head over to urgent care. Chances are, it'll go away on its own. Wake up a week later to 30 pimples? Now you have a skin condition. The pimples are symptoms of something much greater, something that needs to be looked at. In the case of Dennis and O'Hara's, the minor screwups with Dennis's orders were a symptom of a much bigger issue: the way the food was packaged for to-go orders.

Dennis helped identify a problem. By losing a Zombie Loyalist, the restaurant was able to fix the problem and not only win Dennis back but potentially prevent lots of other customers from leaving too. In contrast to the diapers.com story, O'Hara's saw a problem and corrected it. It's easier to do in a small company, harder to do in a bigger one, but there's still no excuse for losing zombies who haves given you multiple chances to keep them.

Nichole Kelly wrote an interesting piece in *Social Media Explorer* about ruining a lifetime of loyalty.[1] In it, she concludes that lifetime loyalists (essentially, Zombie Loyalists) aren't turned away by one giant mistake but rather multiple small problems over a period of time, similar to dying by a thousand cuts.

Nichole counts eight different issues she had with Southwest Airlines over a very short period of time, each one causing her more and more grief and slicing into her loyalty. At any point, Southwest could have reached out and applied pressure to the wound, helping to fix the problem, but it never did. Thus, by the time Nichole had bled out, it was too late to save her; all her loyalty was gone.

It's amazing how many companies get so caught up in the day-to-day running of their business that they don't take the time to poke their heads above their cubicle walls and listen to the wind. Much like the bus company that now makes district managers ride the bus, there are several practices you can implement *today* to keep an eye on your customers and save some zombies before they want to leave.

IS THE LOYAL CUSTOMER WHO USED TO COME IN DAILY ALL OF A SUDDEN DOWN TO ONCE A WEEK OR LESS? REACH OUT.

Several years ago, I joined a local boxing gym as a way to stay in shape. I really enjoyed going, and there's no better way to get rid of your anger and aggression than by repeatedly punching something. About six months in, I faced a six-week business trip, with only three or four days home during that time.

Imagine my surprise when two weeks after my trip had started, I received a personal email from Martin Snow, the owner of Trinity Boxing, wondering why I'd stopped showing up. When I told him that I was on the road for a while, he gave me at least four different gyms I could check out and even went so far as to call the owners of those gyms in different cities to let them know I'd be stopping by for a workout.

Note: I wasn't leaving his gym because I'd had a bad experience, but he didn't know that. So he made it a point to find out.

When you have a customer who comes in all the time and then randomly stops, it should be a priority for you to find out why. With any luck, there's nothing wrong, but if there is, wouldn't you like to know before you've lost the customer entirely?

An added bonus to this method is that a personal reach-out is just that—personal. It's an easy way to get your potentially lost zombie to open up and tell you what's going on—and give you a chance to fix it.

HAS A LOYAL CUSTOMER WHO USED TO SHARE ONLINE CONSTANTLY GONE RADIO SILENT? REACH OUT.

If you're used to seeing someone post every time you serve her a latte, check him in for a flight, or groom her dog, and all of a sudden that stops, you might have a problem. Again, reaching out to ask what's going on isn't just a nice thing to do, it's imperative.

More often than not, it'll be nothing—perhaps the frequent flier is taking a month off to be with a newborn baby. Perhaps the dog wasn't going out so much because it was cold out but will be back in the spring. "I used to take the same spin class every Tuesday and Saturday morning in Union Square," said my friend Emma, "and would check in on Facebook each time. Over time, though, the music kept getting louder and louder in the classes. I wasn't the only one to notice it either. Eventually I just stopped going, after asking that the music be turned down to where it was and being shut out."

About a month after Emma had left her spin classes, she got an email from the manager of the gym—she was missed and he noticed she hadn't tagged the gym online lately; was there anything wrong?

She wrote back and told him that the loud music drove her away and that, despite repeated requests to lower it, nothing changed.

The manager, surprised to hear this, got back to her within a day and comped her next six classes, promising that the music would be back to a level that "wouldn't deafen her."

Emma returned, and hasn't missed a class in over a year.

"In the end, I just wanted someone to hear my request," she said. I didn't think it was unreasonable, and seeing how the classes are fuller than ever when I go, I guess I was right."

Learn to notice when things are out of place, and train your employees to as well. Noticing a sudden lack of a regular zombie could be the difference between losing many of them and/or keeping them all.

You know what saves your zombies from walking? Communication. But you know what pushes them out the door even faster? Communication that doesn't do anything.

If you've ever brought your car back to the dealer for a tune-up, you know what I'm talking about. You get a survey from the dealer that is designed not so much to solve any outstanding problems you might have but to grade the salesperson on his or her work. The problem there, however, is that nothing gets done for you, the customer.

Rather than automate surveys, have actual conversations with your customers. Talk to them like human beings instead of robots. Hear what they're saying, and work with them to find solutions to their problems.

So few companies do this nowadays that the bar is blessedly low for you. Work to push the odds in your favor.

If this book can't convince you to work really hard to save Zombie Loyalists who are about to walk out the door and take with them a lot of business, at the very least perhaps it can convince you that when you *do* lose a zombie, lots of times, it's a symptom of a bigger problem. That's the problem you need to work to fix: the underlying issues of what went wrong that caused you to lose that zombie in the first place.

But with any luck, you're listening to your zombies long before they reach the door.

Onward!

8

YOU FORGOT TO FEED YOUR ZOMBIES!

WHAT TO DO WHEN YOU'VE SCREWED UP AND THERE'S SEVERE DISSENTION IN THE RANKS

Perhaps you stopped nurturing your zombies for whatever reason, and now there's a mutiny. There are even talks of leaving your army for good. Strangely, it's easier to fix a whole group of zombies than it is to fix just one scorned zombie. But you still need to move quickly. Read on for a step-by-step guide to regaining your Zombie Loyalist's love and devotion.

Before we look at some major screwups, let's chat for a second about listening and engaging and how 99 percent of mistakes small companies make involve forgetting how to do the former and not doing anywhere near enough of the latter.

I work with a company in New York City called Simpli.st that lets me figure out what my audience is talking about and the best way to engage them. I asked its CEO, Ron Williams, a man who lives and breathes engagement and listening for his clients day in and day out, why companies screw up as much as they do, to the point where they watch entire armies of Zombie Loyalists walk out the door. In a nutshell, he told me that it's because companies try to feed the same thing to all of their customers, not bothering to learn what makes each one different.

He has a point. I remember getting a letter from the dealership where I'd leased my car. My lease was coming to an end, and the dealer's letter started with "Dear Mr. or Mrs. Shankman." Right there I wasn't leasing another car from the company. When the letter continued with how much "we truly value your business, [CUSTOMERFIRSTNAME]," I was done. Done! The simple act of proofing the email before it went out probably would have landed the company another three-year lease.

Anyhow, Ron makes some good points about listening and engagement, and it's worth the next page or two:

It's no secret that your customers need to be engaged. And talked to. And asked after. And given access. And sometimes just made to feel heard. But the number one mistake made by tons of businesses, movements, and even political campaigns is feeding the same thing to their customers, fans, and followers.

Know your zombies, or ye shall perish!

Knowing who your people are, where they come from, and what motivates them is no longer a nice to have, not just for wealthy companies with big budgets. It's for every single company, big or small, that's building a product, company, movement, or even political campaign. In fact, the 2012 presidential contest demonstrated the value of knowing your people for both candidates. By speaking to smaller and smaller groups of supporters about the particulars of *their* passions, both candidates were able to activate groundswells of supporter-driven campaigning in never-before-seen ways.

So what does this breaking down of customers look like? In bigger companies, the analysis that goes into breaking down your groups of customers into smaller groups, based on shared traits, is called segmentation. At Simpli.st, we just call it common sense. *And now that anyone can do it, you have no excuse not to.* Whether you have 100 customers or 100,000, you owe it to yourself and to your customers to aspire to have each touch be as unique and personalized as humanly and technologically possible.

Why send a marketing email to 100 people talking about something that only 40 of them are likely to care about? Why not take the time to match messaging to basic characteristics like where they live, what they do for a living, and maybe even what they tend to talk about on the web? *All of this information is readily available!* People are raising their hand every day, posting snapshots of what they care about. *Take a moment to tailor your message!*

I'm from Brooklyn and recently became a dog owner. If I follow your brand and/or subscribe to your newsletter and you manage to work "tough Brooklyn puppies" into your post or content, I am 10 to 15X more likely to open and click through. Because you're talking directly to me . . . and the other 50 people like me in your base instead of blasting a middle-of-the-road message that you *hope* works for all 1,000 of your fans, followers, subscribers, and customers. Simple segmentation goes a long way. Moreover, if you can unlock segmentation based upon what people are talking about and doing when they're *not* on your site and bring that perspective into your email segments, you'll win.

In a world that sees all businesses becoming more responsive to the highly specific needs of each customer, it is obvious and harmful when a brand, company, or organization demonstrates that it really knows nothing about a customer. Customers entrust businesses with their data and their dollars. Know your people and engage them the way they want to be engaged. Not all brains are the same.

"Not all brains are the same." If you can remember that, you can avoid 99 percent of the issues you could have that could cause people to leave.

It's ironic that when we talk about building Zombie Loyalists, one of the best ways to actually do that is to treat each zombie like a human being.

Because, let's face it—who doesn't want to be treated like a person, not like a number or just another face in a group?

With that said, let's see what happens when the preceding great suggestions are *not* followed.

When I think back to my college days, one thing always comes to mind—Domino's Pizza. Between my time at Boston University and my years at America Online, the number of pies I put away from that establishment is just . . . Well, I don't want to think about it.

But by 2010, Domino's wasn't doing so well. Its pizza tasted horrible, it was losing market share at an alarming rate, and finding anything positive in any social outpost about the company was pretty difficult.

In short, the chain was in trouble.

Most of the time, when a company realizes it's in trouble, management goes behind closed doors and comes out a year later with a brand-new strategy, focusing on the positives and telling the world why the company is just awesome while never actually acknowledging that there were any problems to begin with.

Domino's could have very easily done that. Instead, management made an odd strategic play: It came out and admitted that, in fact, its product was awful. It admitted that what everyone was saying was right. It admitted that social media was correct and that the people bailing on the company left and right were perfectly justified in doing so.

In short, Domino's admitted it had a serious problem.

According to *The Motley Fool*, Domino's spent millions creating a new pizza from the crust up, expanding its menu offerings, and advertising the process, and the results have been amazing.

Between 2000 and 2013, America's customer satisfaction index score for Domino's Pizza increased from 69 to 81 percent. More important, the company's revenue has also improved significantly.

The commercials showcasing how Domino's planned to improve and what it was doing differently included photos from social media of horrible pizzas, bad delivery, and other problems. Domino's incorporated all of that into a huge marketing blitz and, in the end, saw its stock climb by over 400 percent.[1]

What's my point here? Domino's knew it had a problem that was blatantly showing in the bottom line. Management noticed, took control, and righted the ship.

In the process, it brought back hundreds, if not thousands, of Zombie Loyalists to the church of Domino's and is now consistently leading the pizza delivery pack, not just in the United States but in Europe as well.

I bring this up to make the point that it took Domino's losing a ton of market share, along with the majority of its loyalists, before it realized it needed to do something. The company brought in a new CEO, who turned things around.

Essentially, the whole company got on board with fixing things, because the whole company understood that if it didn't, it might not be a company much longer.

Ironically, it's a lot easier to fix problems and gain back your Zombie Loyalists when it's gotten really, really bad. Because at that point, everyone is ready to accept a turnaround plan.

But when the building is still upright, even with multiple cracks in the foundation, it's a lot harder to implement the changes needed to keep your Zombie Loyalists.

What we're going to nail in this chapter are a bunch of steps that will allow you to talk to your Zombie Loyalists as a group and try and win them back. It's not easy, but it's also not as difficult as you might imagine, if the planets align. In the end, if you can get a handful of zombies back, they'll be your strongest weapon in getting the rest to return as well.

THE EASIEST WAY TO WIN BACK A WHOLE ARMY OF LOYALISTS IN ONE STEP?

Start by Admitting You Were Wrong, as Netflix Did in 2011

Somehow, in 2011, Netflix came to the mistaken conclusion that the best way to get more customers would be to institute a 60 percent price hike and split the company in two. Neither of these ideas turned out to be even close to right, and by mid-2011, Netflix was, according to TheWeek.com, "no more than a punch line."[2]

Knowing that something had to be done to stop the bleeding, Netflix determined that the best fix was twofold: Be honest about the screwups, and change the way it did business.

Netflix launched original programming with the wildly success-ful *House of Cards* and relaunched the cult comedy series *Arrested Development.*

But Jim Cramer of TheStreet.com thinks Netflix also did some-thing big that helped the company even more: It apologized to its audience.

He was quoted as saying "The mea culpa was dismissed by Wall Street, but the customers loved it. The customers came right back. That wasn't in the playbook."[3]

Cramer also argues that Netflix took advantage of people cut-ting the cable cord at the right time.

Long story short, Netflix has more than won back its core Zom-bie Loyalists by doing three things:

1. *Netflix owned the problem.* Management transparently came out and said, "We blew this, we're going to make it better," and then did so.
2. *It went into programming that was able to quickly gain audience share,* thus giving the zombies something to talk about. By the time 2012 rolled around, if you weren't watching Netflix, you were out of the mainstream conversation.
3. *It went after those who felt let down by cable,* which was primarily a younger audience who had no need to pay upward of $80 a month to watch on a TV what they could technically spend $15 a month watching anywhere.

How does this translate to your business?

If you've lost a bunch of zombies virtually overnight, something big must have caused it. Zombies don't just up and leave without a good reason, especially en masse. Find out what it is. Talk to as many customers as you have to, but get to the bottom of it.

Make sure management is on board to let you have as many of these conversations as necessary.

Figure out what you need to change back, or change to, in order to bring them back. Go online and read what they're saying about you. Figure out what key steps need to be taken immediately, what can come next, and what can come next after that.

Be incredibly clear with your messaging. Be as honest and transparent as you can. Again, think about Domino's and Netflix. Both companies apologized and made the changes that needed to be made. They both went from the back of the pack to the front.

THE STORY OF THE ZOMBIE LOYALIST
MOMS WHO ALL LEFT THE POOL

Back in 2009, I was on a panel at South by Southwest, and the subject turned to marketing to moms. I may have made a statement possibly comparing mommy bloggers to the Borg, the alien race in *Star Trek: The Next Generation* known for having one collective consciousness, where all decisions are made through the hive and based solely on whatever is best for the Borg as a race.

Within five minutes, tweets were flying around, talking about how Peter Shankman just compared mommies to aliens, and he's a terrible person.

Keep in mind, I was actually being complimentary—making the point, ironically, that when marketing to a very strong and powerful audience, you need to be careful. One screwup can radiate throughout the collective, and you can lose a whole audience of Zombie Loyalists in a matter of seconds. For reference, see what happened to Motrin when the company talked about how carrying your baby as a fashion accessory could be "painful." Ouch.

Anyway, when all the moms went after me at once, they proved the point brilliantly. Mess with the mommies—or any large, organized collective with a common focal point—at your peril.

So with that said, I want to introduce you to Sarah Savage. Yes, that's her real name, and is there a better name in the entire *world* for a Zombie Loyalist mommy? I mean, come on—sometimes this stuff just writes itself.

Anyhow, Sarah is the perfect example of a Zombie Loyalist who's part of a bigger hive: She's a mom who's active in multiple mom groups, both online and in person. They discuss *everything* related to being a mom, and their recommendations can easily make or break a company.

In her own words, Sarah describes how a collective of Zombie Loyalists can be lost without so much as a moment's notice:

I have witnessed "mommy talk" hurting a small local company's business not once but, in fact, seasonally. There are only a few swim schools in my small city, and there's only one that accepts babies as young as six weeks old. Plus, it has an indoor, heated (think bathtub water), low-chlorinated pool, which sounds like the ideal environment to take a dip with a new baby.

In this city, there are "new mommy" organizations that form new groups bimonthly with moms and babies fresh from the delivery room. Someone in each new group inevitably researches swimming classes for babies, and the next thing you know, the new group's newborns begin classes at this swim school.

At first, the mommies think, "This is great!" It's very exciting to do your first activity with a new baby. Then you realize the pool is scummy with algae overgrowth from the low levels of chlorination and it's seemingly only cleaned on the rare occasion that a baby poops in the water. The place stinks of mildew and stale air and has soggy carpeting. The owner/instructor is friendly, but then she starts opening up to you in "Too-Much-Information"-filled conversations and can occasionally be cluelessly condescending. You begin to dread going to swim class, and soon the moms start commiserating and voicing their concerns at group gatherings.

No one wants to be the first to say how obviously icky the place is, but once someone opens the floodgates, no one can get it out of their minds. The other mommies confirm your own concerns and annoyances about the place. The group pulls together their collective research on other swim school options, and many prepare to jump ship.

Moms start dropping out and heading to the competitions' cleaner, more professional pools. The babies are older now, so they can get into the classes with higher age minimums. That "newborn-friendly" swim school has just lost another round of students to a competitor, and each mom is sure to spread the word about why she pulled her child out. The moms in the same mommy group who hadn't started swim lessons yet will avoid this school when they do start.

From what I've seen from friends with children of varying ages, the migration away from this particular school occurs over and over again. Each new mommy group formation brings new students who eventually, the majority at least, leave. The school is lucky to have so much business, which is ultimately by default because of the six-week-old age minimum and the fact that it's catering to new moms whose support group is filled with other new moms and therefore haven't yet heard the truth of the school's downfalls.

I haven't seen the owner of the school do much to chase after fleeing customers. From the outside, it seems like she doesn't have a clue as to why people leave. If she did, she'd be crazy not to fix the problems. I think surveying students for anonymous feedback would bring the school's downfalls to light for the owner. Let's face it, are people ever truly honest if it isn't anonymous? The owner is missing out on an opportunity to learn her school's weaknesses, how to keep students long term, and ultimately grow her business. I assure you that the new moms who experience her business have no qualms about sharing it with anyone who will listen.

LESSON: If you work in any industry with a "collective" (think moms or avid video gamers or classic car enthusiasts), you need to be even more careful, and more aware of everything that's being said. It takes so little to lose one, and if they're part of a closely networked collective, you can lose them all.

The key takeaway here, as in so many other instances, is simply to *listen more*. Being able to listen and make adjustments on the fly will almost *always* stop a collective of Zombies from walking out. (Or at least slow them down enough so you can try and right the ship.)

HOW DO YOU GET ZOMBIE LOYALISTS OF YOUR OWN IF YOU DON'T HAVE ANY? BREAK THE RULES AND STEAL THEM BACK

The Story of the New No-Contract, No-Roaming T-Mobile

It's no secret that Americans hate their mobile phone companies. They rank right up there with "the stuff you scrape off your shoe" on those "most hated companies" lists that come out all the time. But for the longest time, there wasn't much of a difference among mobile phone companies other than coverage, and when one went bad (think AT&T not having enough bandwidth when the first iPhone came out), you simply switched to another one. The next one might have been just as bad on billing and draconian contracts, but at least you got two bars of service in your bedroom.

Then T-Mobile (which, at the time, was to mobile providers what FOX TV was to NBC in the late 1980s—far from a threat) did something revolutionary: It started breaking the rules.

Don't want a contract? Cool, no contract, pay as you go. Travel overseas? No worries—we won't charge you roaming fees (which on other carriers could be the cost of a mortgage payment).

Instead, T-Mobile took the line of "We hear you—you're the customer, you want better, you deserve better, we're going to give it to you."

While that was easy to say, would customers really switch? At first, it seemed like they would, and T-Mobile started seeing a slight uptick in customers who were at the end of their contracts with other carriers and just wanted something better. It was a small number at first, but it was telling: Customers wanted to be treated better.

T-Mobile, realizing an opportunity to create a true breed of Zombie Loyalists, did something that, on the surface, sounded beyond insane: It offered to buy customers of other carriers out of their contracts, paying their early termination fee if they'd switch over to T-Mobile.

Within days, a whole new breed of Zombie Loyalists was born and raised into a collective of happy users who would stop at nothing to tell everyone else how awesome the new carrier was.

TheStreet.com reported on it with amazement in early 2014: "After years of market share losses and declining subscribers, T-Mobile added 1.6 million customers in the fourth-quarter of 2013."[4]

That's 1.6 million new Zombie Loyalists who come to the company knowing that they don't need a contract and they won't get hit with roaming charges—exactly what they hated about their old mobile providers.

Sometimes, when you need to create a zombie army, doing something unheard of, or even crazy, could just be the way to go.

NOTHING INVIGORATES A SMALL ARMY OF ZOMBIE LOYALISTS MORE THAN BRINGING THEM MILLIONS OF POTENTIAL NEW RECRUITS

The Apple Turnaround

No book on Zombie Loyalists would be complete without a mention of Apple Computer—a story we all know, but it's always worth repeating.

Steve Jobs founded Apple in 1976 and is credited with creating one of the world's first personal computers, which actually for a little bit competed directly with IBM's PC computers running Microsoft.

The 1984 launch of Macintosh is, to this day, credited as one of the world's best launches of any product, complete with the two-minute Super Bowl spot called simply "1984."

But by 1985, Apple's board didn't think Steve Jobs was mature enough to handle the company's growth, and it kicked him out, replacing him with John Sculley, formerly of Pepsi. Sculley pushed

Jobs out completely, and the man who founded Apple was removed from the very company he created.

The next years were hard on Apple and, more important, on Apple Zombie Loyalists, of whom I was one. Any idea what it's like going into a store for software (back when they still had stores that sold software) and seeing 400 shelves of PC products and one shelf of Apple products?

By 1997, Apple had gone through two CEOs and massive lay-offs, and even its most stoic Zombie Loyalists were rushing for the exits. Then the company did something amazing: It turned to its founder and asked him back.

(As an aside, you have to imagine that the swagger-walk Steve Jobs did that first day he came back to his company would rival anything any Super Bowl MVP could ever do.)

Anyhow, he came back, and in 1998, he launched the iMac in multiple colors, proving that computers could be fun and quirky and still wildly powerful. As people started flocking to this "new" company, the original Zombie Loyalists started waking up and welcoming new zombies into their army.

Finally, in 2000, Apple launched the iPod, and the zombies went insane. Not only did Apple revolutionize how music and content was made, bought, used, and consumed, but it also created Zombie Loyalists with every purchase: Who didn't want the cool new iPod? Then the iPhone? Then the iPad? Then the MacBook Air?

Walk into any Starbucks now, and every table has four Mac-Book Airs on it. But even more, walk into any airport lounge, where the PC has been the businessman's computer of choice since laptops were invented, and note how many Macs you see.

There may be no more loyal zombie than an Apple zombie, and even with the passing of Steve Jobs, the future looks incredibly bright for the company.

LESSON: When Apple started coming back, what moved the company along were good products and new thinking. But the zombies certainly helped. Walk into an Apple store today, and everyone there (especially the people who don't actually work there) is happy to answer any questions you have. It truly is a cult following, led by Zombie Loyalists.

Loyalty is everything. Let your fans tell the world how great you are, let your zombies show them. In the end, it's up to you to put out a great product and fix the product if your zombies are starting to leave. But the loyalty that's built should never be wasted. Feed your zombies, and, even if times are lean, they'll stick with you.

IT'S ABOUT THE COFFEE, STUPID

How Starbucks Won Back Millions of Caffeinated Zombie Loyalists Looking for Their Morning Buzz

The Starbucks logo is probably one of the most ubiquitous in the universe, but back in 2007, its over 15,000 stores were cannibalizing each other, and the brand had lost its focus, with diversifications that included music, coffee accessories, and random food items. Management, and CEO Jim Donald, completely forgot what made Starbucks what it was: coffee!

While Starbucks was trying to become a media company, McDonald's started fiercely competing against it, reformulating its coffee and going heavy on the promotion, taking tons and tons of Starbucks Zombie Loyalists over to the Golden Arches.

By 2007, Starbucks stock was falling rapidly, as more and more coffee purists were getting their fix anywhere else. CEO Howard Schultz came back and massively cut costs, restoring the coffeehouse feel that the chain maintains today.

The company also focused on making sure employees were happy, with good wages and health insurance, taking the job of barista from a college joke to the start of a potentially decent career with a growing multinational company.

The zombies returned, and if you walk into Starbucks today, you'd guess they never left. It's been estimated that over half the start-ups in America today have called their local Starbucks "their office" at one point in their life cycle, and Starbucks still remains one of the top meeting places in the country, for everything from entre-preneurs to running groups.

LESSONS: The easiest way to lose Zombie Loyalists is to wander too far from what brought them to you in the first place. If zombies came to you for brains and all of a sudden you're serving quiche, they're going to leave. Do what you know, and even if you introduce new things, never let them overshadow that original mission. Core competencies are core for a reason. Never forget that.

Second, be true to who you are. Just because another company has a market share that you want, don't change everything to try to get it. That's like working really hard to get one woman to let you take her to the dance and, as soon as you get there, looking around for someone better. If you try too hard to get the audience you want, you're insulting the audience you have, and the audience you have will *always* do a better job of getting you the audience you want than you alone will.

Focus on the Zombie Loyalists you have to build the Zombie Loyalists you want. They'll appreciate you more, and bring you your new customers.

It occurs to me that I can't sit here and talk all about screwups, being honest, owning it, and the like, and not share one of my worst corporate screwups as well.

THE CONFERENCE CALL THAT WENT BAD

And How We Came Out of It Okay without Breaking Down, Losing Our Minds, or Drinking Heavily

You never want to hear the words "uh-oh." It's so rare that any-thing good ever comes immediately after "uh-oh." You never hear "Uh-oh, I just won the lottery," or "Uh-oh, that supermodel said she wants to date me."

No, "uh-oh" is usually followed by "the server just went down," or "we just lost our number-two engine," or "did I forget to pack my parachute?"

So it was with very little happiness that I uttered "uh-oh" in February 2009. I was holding a conference call for about 700 or so people, all of whom had paid $50 per head to attend. The subject was how best to pitch the media, and speakers included reporters from the *Wall Street Journal, New York Times,* and *LA Times.*

I'd been promoting the call for a few months. It was definitely a big deal, and we'd gotten a bit of media coverage about it, since everyone wants to know how to best get their story into the press.

Two p.m. EST came, and the call started. I'd received an instant message saying that we'd broken 700 people, the largest number we'd ever had on these calls. And those were just 700 people who'd paid for the call—who knew how many were listening in conference rooms, around tables, in offices, wherever? This was huge, and I was psyched. Worried, but psyched.

I made brief introductions, introducing each reporter and asking them to talk a bit about themselves. Then, about five minutes into the call, I started with my prepared questions.

As we got to question number three, probably about ten minutes into the one-hour call, I heard a slight, one-second hiccup on the call quality. I guess that's the best way to describe it. Just a small blip, like we lost the signal for a second.

No big deal. The call kept going. But then another blip. And then another. And then, within 20 seconds, we no longer heard the call. Instead, we heard nothing but beeps and blips. We'd lost the call.

I was shell-shocked. I vaguely remember saying something like "Obviously, the call can't continue with the quality listed, so we'll regroup and we'll make the call happen again as soon as we figure out what happened."

Then I went out onto my office's balcony and wished like hell that I hadn't quit smoking several years earlier, because right then, I wanted a cigarette more than I ever had in my life.

So at this point, I had two choices . . . I was already seeing what was going on via Twitter, and mostly it was tweets ending with the hashtag #FAIL.

I could lose tons of customers, tons of clients, tons of respect, and tons of brand equity while refunding only those who asked for their money back.

Or I could face the music, own it, and make things right.

Not really that much of a choice, when you think about it.

First, I had to understand what had happened—not only technically (in fact, why the call died was the least of my worries), but I had to put myself in my customers' heads—all 700 or so of them who just paid $50 for 10 minutes of information and 50 minutes of static.

We promised something to our audience. They paid for it based on that promise. We couldn't deliver it, and we now had to make good.

As I said, a quick scan of Twitter told me the story. "Can anyone else get sound from the call?" "Call quality sucks!" "What happened?" "@petershankman, WTF? We paid $50 for this?"

Okay. They were pissed off, and rightly so. They were confused, and rightly so. They felt cheated, and rightly so.

I had one thing to do: *Get another call as soon as possible.* To do that, I connected with all the reporters on the call, silently praying that they could all make the call at the same time tomorrow. The fates smiled on me, as they all could.

Then I called the conference call company and told the agent I'd yell at them later, but right now, they had to make the call work, exactly 23 hours from now. I may have thrown in a note about how my audience of 75,000 people on Twitter and 100,000 people on Facebook would know that I'd blame the company if this wasn't fixed.

Whether that was true or not (it wasn't), I had to say it. The call had to happen, and it had to be *flawless.*

Then, after all the steps were taken, I had to respond publicly. *Some helpful hints about responding:*

- Take five deep, cleansing breaths before you type anything. Your adrenaline is already through the roof. You must calm down before you post anything. (To quote Lloyd Dobler in the film *Say Anything,* "YOU MUST CHILL! YOU MUST CHILL!")

- Make sure your laptop is *not* connected to the Internet until you've finished your response, walked away, come back, looked again, shown it to a trusted friend (and an attorney, if necessary), and are truly, truly ready to send. There's nothing worse than putting a mistake out there on top of a mistake.

- Finally, it's business. Apologize all you want, even own the mistake personally, but *don't make it personal.* No one cares that your cat threw up the same day that your pants ripped and then the call went down. It's not about you. It's about your customers.

Following those rules, we issued this on my blog:

RESPONSE FROM PETER SHANKMAN AND HARO REGARDING TODAY'S CONFERENCE CALL
First things first:

Today's HARO "How to Pitch Business Reporters" will be rescheduled for tomorrow, Thursday, February 19th, at 2pm (14:00) EST.

Now then:

To my esteemed panelists, and to all the audience members listening in: I'm truly sorry. While the problem was caused by technical issues, the fact is, I organized the call, I promoted it, my panel convened at my request, and the audience paid for it on my recommendation. As such, I accept full responsibility for today's SNAFU, regardless of what caused it.

We don't know exactly what happened. What I do know is that I've used Conference Call University for our previous two calls, without any problems at all. We've never had so much as a blip of trouble on either of the previous calls, and had no reason to expect any different. Obviously, that's not what happened today.

I truly apologize to each and every one of you, and I vow to make this right.

Tomorrow's conference call will take place at 2 pm EST, just like today's did. CCU will be responsible for giving out the conference call dial-in number for the audience members. For the panel members, I will call each of you personally an hour before the call and give you the dial-in numbers.

One final time: I'm truly sorry. For those who can't make the call tomorrow, I will personally send you an mp3 of the call the second it finishes saving.

Thank you all for your understanding. If I can answer any further questions, you know I'm available to you via email—peter@shankman.com, via twitter @petershankman, or via a cup of coffee if we're in the same city.

—Peter Shankman
15:00, 02/18/09

And that was it. To the point, simple, and quick. I apologized, I explained what happened, but, most important, I explained to my audience exactly how I was going to fix it and what would happen if said fix didn't work for any specific audience member.

I knew I had to work fast. The tweets were already going out about how people wanted refunds, were pissed off, and so on. So the post went up, I tweeted it out, then I waited.

At some point, you need to know you've done all you can. Then you just have to wait.

Within two minutes, the first comments started appearing on the blog, and almost all of them were positive!

Kary Delaria wrote:

February 18th, 2009 at 3:35 pm
Thank you, Peter. This is a stellar example of how to react when everything hits the fan, even when it was clearly beyond your control. I continue to have the utmost respect for you and am looking forward to trying the call again tomorrow!

Best,
Kary

Amy wrote:

February 18th, 2009 at 3:54 pm
Really impressed with both of you (Peter and Conference Call University)—
perfect handling of this situation. Don't beat yourselves up. :0)

Sue Jacques wrote:

February 18th, 2009 at 5:11 pm
Peter/Marty,
Thank you for handling this unfortunate event with dignity and grace. You took
ownership and accountability and showed all of us all how to handle such
circumstances with absolute professionalism. Well done! See you tomorrow . . .

Respectfully,
Sue Jacques

Sure, we lost a few people, but we actually gained more, via people who couldn't make the original call. End result? We saved our audience, we saved our brand.

I won't lie: For about four hours, you did *not* want to be in the same room with me. But by the time the problem resolved itself 24 hours later, something else had happened on the Internet, and the world had moved on.

That's key as well: Do what you can do to fix your mistakes, but know that there will *always* be something that grabs people's attention and takes the white-hot spotlight of shame off of you. Hopefully, it's in conjunction with your apology, and you've built such a loyal audience of zombies to begin with that the damage isn't too severe, but even if it is, know that it's never fatal, and it's never forever.

The nice thing about having Zombie Loyalists is that they're loyal. When you do screw up (and you will), your chances of getting your business back into favor with your zombies is determined by two things: how well you do in correcting your mistake and also how well you've done in the past at keeping your Zombie Loyalists happy. Happy Zombie Loyalists are much more willing to forgive than customers who were already on the fence to begin with.

Like most things, there's no one "moment" when everything goes to hell. Chances are, it started a long time ago. So focus on making things right from day one, focus on breeding Zombie Loyalists from the start, so that when the day comes when you *have* done something wrong, you won't have that far to go to get everyone back on your side.

9

ZOMBIE LOYALIST HACKS

MORE TIPS AND TRICKS TO MAINTAINING ZOMBIE LOYALTY

There have been reports, from field scientists studying Zombie Loyalists in their natural habitat, that zombies occasionally get bored. When that happens, their loyalty starts to fade. In a few rare cases, Zombie Loyalists can stop feeding altogether and look for a new source of food. This is obviously very, very dangerous to your business. In this chapter, we'll discuss ways of hacking the brains of your best Zombie Loyalists to ensure that they stay with you, never get bored, and continue to infect new customers for you.

PEOPLE GET BORED. IT'S HUMAN NATURE.
BRING RANDOM AMAZEMENT INTO NORMAL
SITUATIONS TO PREVENT BOREDOM AND
KEEP YOUR ZOMBIE LOYALISTS HAPPY

I remember a hot, hot summer day when I was about eight years old. I didn't want to go out and play; it was too hot. But there was nothing to do inside. Instead of reading a book or helping with a chore, I took it upon myself to make sure both my parents, in different parts of the house, knew exactly how bored I was, how boring it was in the house, how hot it was outside, how unhappy I really was, and how miserable I was going to be, obviously for the rest of my entire hot, boring, unhappy life.

Finally, after a solid hour of my doing nothing but complaining, my father looked up, reached over for the super-large glass of ice water he'd been sipping, stood up, and dumped the entire glass on my head.

"There, now you have something to do," he said to me, as I stood there with ice water running down my shirt and into my shorts.

To this day, he swears he doesn't remember doing that, but I have a great memory. I know this happened.

The point? Everybody gets bored from time to time. We get into ruts; we do the same thing over and over every day, with no passion. When that happens, we look for something new to do.

The same thing can happen with your business. Over time, people can get bored. They can look for something new. If there's no excitement left, there's very little reason for them to stay.

The good thing, though, is that the excitement doesn't need to be massive, nor does it have to be expensive. Let's spend this chapter talking about what other companies have done to counteract Zombie Loyalist boredom as well as guarantee that they stay in their zombies' minds.

THE HALF-HOUR EARLY-MORNING PHONE CALL

This story has been passed down for years and to this day is still one of my all-time favorite stories about a CEO making a change.

When Barry Diller joined Paramount pictures in the late 1970s, it wasn't exactly the greatest movie studio in Hollywood. Barry had his work cut out for him. Some people, in fact, told him that going to Paramount was essentially career suicide, and he should reconsider.

But the lure of running a major motion picture studio was too strong to turn down, and Barry took the job.

The story goes that the one thing Barry did every morning, without fail, for half an hour, was call ten random people in his Rolodex, just to say hi.

He never tried to sell them on anything, nor did he ever try to pitch them. He just called to say hi.

Remember, this was back in the days of rotary phones. It wasn't as easy a process as saying "Siri, please call someone."

Yet he did it anyway, every day, and if you were in Barry's Rolodex, then you got a call from the president of Paramount Pictures about four times a year, just saying hi, asking what was up, inquiring about your family.

No selling.

When you had a movie you wanted green-lit, or you had a client you wanted signed to a five-picture deal, or you wanted to get anything done in Hollywood, you had two choices: You could work the phone tree at any studio but Paramount and hope to get lucky, or . . .

You could call Barry back.

Barry Diller, simply put, was top of mind. He was the first thing you thought about when you thought about Hollywood, because at some point in the last 12 weeks, he'd called you to say hi.

Under Barry's tenure, Paramount turned around and, to this day, is one of the top-performing movie studios in Hollywood. Paramount's success continued long after Diller left, with films like *Footloose, Pretty in Pink, Flashdance, An Officer and a Gentleman,* and *Trading Places.*

Barry knew that the secret to staying top of mind and making sure your zombies stay loyal and don't get bored was to simply check in and say hi, so he did, and the results speak for themselves.

Let's discuss some other ways you can stay top of mind to your customers and clients from companies doing it right now.

Remember, the next steps aren't self-promotion. Rather, they're genuine acts of kindness, help, or just plain fun. If the results *from* these steps increase business or reenergize your Zombie Loyalists, well, then, that's just a double win.

FLOWERS WHEN THEY'RE REALLY NEEDED ARE EVEN BETTER WHEN THEY'RE UNEXPECTED

Randi Milner had used Rent the Runway, a service that lets you rent high-priced fashion for special events, for an event with her fiancé. A few days before the event, she returned the dress and, under "reason for return," put "fiancé just broke up with me, won't need it anymore."

Any company full of somewhat decent folk would return her money with no questions asked, which is exactly what Rent the Runway did. But what made Randi a Zombie Loyalist was what happened a couple weeks later:

"On Valentine's Day, I got a beautiful bouquet of flowers from Rent the Runway, with a note that read 'Happy It's His Loss Day!' It was the most touching thing, and guaranteed my loyalty to Rent the Runway."

You know that Randi is now a Zombie Loyalist for life, armed with a great story to share whenever the subject of clothing is brought up.

I can also tell you from personal experience that my assistant continually raves about the service she receives from Rent the Runway. That I remember this, when I have no need to even know who the company is, speaks volumes about how well the company treats her.

LESSON: Reaching out to your zombies with a much-needed smile is never a bad idea. The cost of whatever you do will be minimal compared to the loyalty you'll receive and the friends they'll bring in.

Bring random amazement into normal situations.

KINDNESS IS LIKE A FERTILITY TREATMENT FOR BREEDING ZOMBIE LOYALISTS

Kim McMahon was surprised to see that the person she had hired to shovel the snow from her property had just stopped by for no reason, until he told her that he'd heard from a neighbor that Kim had recently lost her husband. He wanted to see how she was doing and if she needed anything.

Touched as she was, she was more amazed when, after asking him if he knew anyone who could remove a few small trees from her yard, he looked at them and said, "Oh, I can do that," and proceeded to do it.

The man continued to stop by every once in a while just to check in, and when Kim mentioned that she was looking for someone to replace her driveway, he whipped out his phone and called someone he trusted. When the job was done, the company told her that she was receiving a "friend" discount, because her snow removal person had asked them to take care of her.

Kim goes out of her way to recommend both companies whenever she can.

LESSON: The value of kindness is highly underrated by most companies today, which is funny, because it's been proven over and over again that even the smallest kindness can generate tremendous extra revenue, not to mention lots of good karma for you and your business, if you believe in that sort of thing.

The level of a company's kindness can be traced back pretty easily to your hiring practices. If you hire good, caring people, they'll bring those traits with them to the job every single day. Almost nothing breeds Zombie Loyalists more efficiently than kindness.

How can you encourage your employees, and yourself, to practice random acts of kindness? (This is another one of those things that needs to come from the top down, by the way.)

Scott Sanders tells the story of his father, a huge fan of the author Jeffrey Gitomer:

> My favorite example is sales author Jeffrey Gitomer. My dad is a big fan of his work, and for my dad's sixtieth birthday, I wrote to Gitomer's office to see if there was a special gift pack or something unadvertised I could purchase as a special treat.
>
> In response, they asked for a name and address and basically said "we'll take care of it!" They sent a huge care package and tickets to one of his seminars and [a] meeting with Gitomer—all at no cost for a fan. Probably $400 or more in value. They gained a fan for life from my dad, which he already was, plus my siblings and I, who were blown away by this amazing act of generosity and general awesomeness.

Bring random amazement into normal situations.

IT'S THE SMALLEST THINGS (NO, LITERALLY)
THAT MAKE ZOMBIE LOYALIST FAMILIES

If I could tell a company to keep a few types of "special" gifts on hand for Zombie Loyalists, they would undoubtedly be baby onesies and cat/dog toys.

Let's face it: How many companies have given you USB thumb drives or Post-it notes? First off, who really needs them? Second, who cares? You know they bought a thousand of them and send them out to anyone. There's no "special" in them, nothing that screams "We love you for loving us!"

The technology available to us today, in the form of social networks and real-time alerts, makes it almost embarrassing that companies don't better track what's going on in the lives of their most special guests.

Between Twitter, Facebook, and Google alerts, it doesn't take much to learn more about customers and turn them into Zombie Loyalists, or keep Zombie Loyalists happy and top of mind. In fact, it's downright easy.

Uber is one of the fastest-growing sharing-economy companies in the world, a revolutionary take on getting a cab. Instead of standing in the rain with your hand raised, you simply tap a few times on an app on your phone, and a car shows up. It's brilliant in its simplicity.

While Uber has had more than its share of missteps, it's growing and creating Zombie Loyalists every single day. The service itself is easy to use and tremendously beneficial, considering it's only a few bucks more than a regular taxi would charge and still cheaper than a regular high-end car service. But what truly separates Uber and helps it breed its zombies is its attention to specific customers, even when those customers *aren't* in an Uber car.

When Dave Donahue, a marketing and communications professional, discovered Uber, he was hooked, and he routinely uses the service in multiple cities.

A little while back, Dave and his wife welcomed their first child. Within a week, Dave got home to find an Uber-branded onesie for his child, along with a note of congratulations.

He was floored and, of course, immediately took photos and shared the news with the world. He's also that much more of a Zombie Loyalist now, and he converts friends whenever possible.

There's something about a company humanizing itself, as I mentioned a few chapters ago, and nothing humanizes a company in a Zombie Loyalist's eyes more than noticing a truly monumental event in the customer's life and congratulating accordingly.

Uber isn't the only one to hop on the baby zombie train. (And seriously, doesn't *Baby Zombie Train* sound like an awesome B movie?)

When my daughter was born just about a year ago, Starwood Preferred Guest, the loyalty program of Westin, Sheraton, W Hotels, and the like, knew about it because they follow me throughout social media.

Sure enough, this showed up at my door a few weeks later:

As a frequent traveler and SPG Zombie Loyalist, knowing that my kid is probably the youngest SPG member really kind of thrills me, in a travel-geek type of way. She's worn that onesie many, many times.

My best friend, Ty Francis, is also a heavy frequent flier. He's loyal to Virgin the same way I'm loyal to United. So it was a thrill beyond words for him when he was able to meet Sir Richard Branson at an event for Virgin frequent fliers in New York a few years back. Ty attended the event with his wife, Alayna, who at the time was noticeably pregnant.

Sir Richard picked up on this, posing for pictures with the two of them and cradling Alayna's stomach while jokingly attempting to push Ty out of the picture.

Fast forward to a few weeks after Ty's daughter is born. Ty just happens to be reading Sir Richard's blog and notices a post with the headline "Our Youngest Virgin Atlantic Member!"

Photos of the event and even one of Ty and his wife and daughter adorned the page, filled with congratulations from Sir Richard himself.

Needless to say, everyone who knows Ty knew about this immediately from Ty himself, and Ty's zombie loyalism to Virgin was cemented for generations of Francises to come. You can read the blog post here: http://bit.ly/SerenVASRB.

You've simply got to know your best customers. Really take the time to get to know them. Talk to them. Take five minutes out of each day to connect with at least one of them. See what's going on in their world that excites them, and find out how you can occasionally make it even better for them. SPG didn't have to send me a shirt, Virgin didn't have to give Ty a shout-out, and Uber didn't have to give Dave a onesie. They all did it because they care about their customers, and more important, they know the value of a happy Zombie Loyalist.

Bring random amazement into normal situations.

"ANY BOOK WHERE YOU CAN USE THE TERM 'ZOMBIE HACKS' HAS TO HAVE SOME VALUE, RIGHT?"—THE AUTHOR PITCHING HIS EDITOR ON WHY THIS BOOK SHOULD MAKE IT TO PRINT

Beth is a private investigator, with the great Twitter name of @The BlondePI. When she works fraud investigations and she's finished her surveillance of her insurance claimant, she'll submit her video and report. If she doesn't hear from the insurance company with authorization for more surveillance, she'll do it anyway and follow up to the company with a note: "No charge, just wanted you to know what she's been up to."

She stays top of mind with the insurance company and is always its first call for new clients. Added bonus? She usually gets more work on the initial claimant anyway. A win-win!

I feel it's important to highlight something here: It's not written in stone that you take this kind of action only for Zombie Loyalists. Quite the opposite; it's just as beneficial to do this for first-time customers or even those who have yet to *become* customers, as exemplified here by Jasmine Trillos-Decarie, a marketing director of a law firm in Boston:

> When Del Frisco's moved into my firm's neighborhood they called me up to let us know they were going to bring lunch in for my team. They put out an amazing spread without us having ever hosted an event at any of their locations. More importantly, it was not followed up by any sales calls. It was their way of getting to know their neighbors, at least some of us. Smart.

Of course, you're thinking to yourself, "That wasn't them being nice, that was advertising to a company that could hire them to cater a meal!" to which I say, "What's the difference?" The company wasn't selling in an obvious in-your-face, buy-from-us way. It offered a service that everyone needs anyway (lunch), and offered it for free. Was that an introduction to Del Frisco's? Of course! But it's also a free lunch, which actually was free. How is that disingenuous in the slightest? And isn't it better than an ad shoved under the law firm's door or, worse, cold calls to the marketing director trying to sell her?

Simple things. It's always the simple things. From Kevin Strawbridge in Plano, Texas, more proof of that principle:

> Anytime I go into my local Jersey Mike's in Plano, TX, with my kids the owner always stops by the table and gives the kids a cookie. These are the cookies they sell, not some token freebie. It is unsolicited (and still unexpected—i.e., if we did not get one, it would not change my going there 2X per week) but makes such a statement. This local business (even though a franchise) totally gets making a personal connection with the patrons. Beyond the customer satisfaction, the company has also created a huge philanthropic impact for the community with hundreds of thousands of dollars raised. Like the philanthropy, little tokens add up to a big win over the long term.

UPGRADES ARE BEST WHEN YOU LEAST EXPECT THEM

Did you know that the Chicago Symphony Orchestra randomly picks a few attendees at each concert and gives them a seat upgrade, a CD of the orchestra, and free parking coupons, just because? There's no reason why, and the orchestra doesn't know the people who are being upgraded—it could be a lifelong member or a first-time attendee. But the orchestra is known for it, and it brings happiness to people who might now have even more of a reason to come back. It's the simplest thing to do, it takes about ten seconds, but the stories that come out of it resonate for years. "Remember that time we went on our second date and . . ." "Yeah, Dad, we know, the CSO upgraded you. We've heard it a thousand times."

Bring random amazement into normal situations.

You know what that does? That creates Zombie Loyalists.

You don't need to do anything super-special. You don't need to deliver a steak to the airport. You need to have employees who love what they do and take pride in it and actually *want* to make things better—for their coworkers, for their customers, for the world, and, yes, even for themselves, and they realize that doing all four can work symbiotically.

I spoke with Ralph Vick, the general manager of the Ritz-Carlton Lodge, Reynolds Plantation, about this.

Ralph believes that the concept of bringing random amazement into normal situations starts with the employees and seeps into the culture.

"We don't *hire* employees," he told me. "We *select them*. We look for a gift—a set of morals and values that our parents gave us about how people should be treated, and we hire people who demonstrate that they have them.

"We look for a unique set of service characteristics to make an outstanding employee that not everyone has," he says.

It has to start with your people. The right people strengthen your corporate culture; the wrong ones weaken it. It's why the employee selection process at the Ritz-Carlton is so stringent. They only want employees (or ladies and gentlemen, as they are called) who will strengthen that corporate culture.

Ralph also told me that after the company selects, trains, and orients employees, it gets out of their way and lets them do their job. "The employee knows that they're empowered to move heaven and earth to satisfy the guest and create 'wow' moments for them through every interaction."

His next statement, though, was the most important to me: "We let them do their job and trust that they'll do it the right way. This empowers them to become the decision makers, and our employees feed on that. It's very powerful."

Bring random amazement into normal situations.

Did you know that when Amazon first launched, it sent coffee cups to its first customers, thanking them for their loyalty? This was in 1994 and 1995.

I still have mine. That should tell you something right there.

David Roher ran a Gloria Jean's Coffee store in Westchester, New York, back in the 1990s (pre-Twitter). He tells stories of walking around the store and asking one question to every guest: "Is your drink perfect?"

If they said it wasn't, it didn't matter what the problem was, it was remade fresh on the spot, no charge. It didn't matter if they were 99 percent done with it, it was remade fresh on the spot. He mentions with a bit of deserved pride that his was the busiest shop on the East Coast.

Remember in the beginning of the book, I told you about the SCOTTeVEST and my love for them? (I also told you I was on the company's advisory board. I'm saying it again for full-full disclosure.)

Anyhow, Scott Jordan, the founder, is known as a bit of a free spirit. He says what he feels, and it occasionally causes him some grief. But he's one of the most honest, genuine, and simply decent people I've ever met.

Awhile back, he did a Reddit AMA. (For those who don't know, an AMA is short for "Ask Me Anything," where you sit and answer questions from members of Reddit, a very popular online forum, on any topic, usually related to what you do for a living.)

One customer mentioned that he had lost a lot of weight and was saving up to replace the SCOTTeVEST products he owned in his new size. Scott made up a new promotion on the spot, offering the man a special discount to get smaller-size SeV and congratulating him on the weight lost.

The customer was overjoyed and, of course, bought the products and told the world.

My question to you is this: Why *wouldn't* you do this? If a small, one-time percentage off one item is such a costly bottom-line inconvenience compared to the Zombie Loyalty you'll get from it, you might need to focus on increasing your margins.

As Scott puts it:

By going above and beyond the average attention to customer needs, you create opportunities to make SCOTTeVEST more than a product, and you begin to build brand loyalty when you connect with their personal lives on a deeper level. Being "nice" means really listening to your customers and reading deeper into their needs and uses for our products and taking our interactions with them a step further into their personal lives beyond just a transactional interaction.

Bring random amazement into normal situations.

"WE DON'T HAVE A CUSTOMER SERVICE DEPARTMENT, BECAUSE WE'RE A CUSTOMER SERVICE COMPANY"

If you're any type of sports fan, you've no doubt heard of Steiner Sports. The leader in sports memorabilia, it's known around the globe for those ridiculously hard-to-find presents for the sports nut in your life, whether it's your dad who loves golf, or the ultimate Mets fan you're married to, or even your kid and his idolization of Derek Jeter. If it's sports related and you need it, Steiner Sports will have it.

Steiner knows, though, that it's in the business of making people happy, and some of its items are downright pricey. With that in mind, Steiner's CEO, Brandon Steiner, believes that it's not enough to just have a customer service department. You need to be a customer service company, through and through.

Through email, Brandon told me about the philosophy he's built into the corporate culture at Steiner Sports.

Before I eliminated the customer service "department" at Steiner Sports, whenever there was a problem, everyone just passed that along to one or two specific people, and in the end, this was extremely ineffective. I decided to sit all of my employees down and explain that they had to have a true understanding of who their customers were. To do that, my employees had to be completely involved in the process of seeing things through directly with the customers.

While I used to think that customer service was important, I've come to the realization that customer service is *everything,* especially these days, for obvious reasons. With the advent of social media, customers have a direct and diverse set of ways to complain. Customer complaints are no longer just a one-on-one phone conversation. Someone could literally reach millions of people from the palm of their hand. That can be an extremely dangerous asset to your business. And, don't forget that negative consumer sentiment is expensive. Nobody wants to buy the next thing if they're not happy with the last thing. When their friends all know about it, they won't buy it either.

Of course, while many customers may turn to social media to talk about a negative experience they've had with [a] company, there's also an opportunity to make something positive very quickly. Never before could you have your entire customer base literally at your fingertips, but now you can. Use it to your advantage. I always say that the stupidest thing you can do in business is not making a mistake, but making a mistake twice. With today's technology, you have no excuse.

Since we've transitioned away from a customer service "department" at Steiner Sports, we believe in one simple rule-of-thumb that dictates our customer service policy: treat your customer as you would treat your mother.

As you would treat your mother. That's powerful. Who wouldn't pick up a quick bouquet of flowers on their way to see Mom, or give her a quick call to say hi?

Bring random amazement into normal situations.

If you own a flower shop, can you empower employees to occasionally send some flowers to a customer you haven't heard from in a while?

If you own any place where the board of health doesn't allow pets, can you put doggie water bowls outside in the summer months so as they wait for their owners, they can have a drink?

If you run an airline, can you empower your employees to note body language, and offer someone a free drink or even simply a smile if they look stressed?

If you own a taxi service, can you invest in five-dollar cell phone charging cables that drivers can plug in so that every passenger who uses your cars can charge up as they're being driven?

If you own a hot dog cart business, can you empower your employees to have some fun with the ketchup and mustard?

If you own a spa, can you empower employees to subtly ask their guests if they're celebrating anything, and if they are, let them do something extra?

If you own a contracting company, can you invest in a digital camera for your workers so they can document the job and present an album as a gift?

If you own a deli franchise, can you start following people who come into your store on Twitter? And if they tweet they're freezing, can you send the occasional free bowl of soup?

If you own an ice cream shop, can you offer discounts for anyone coming in after a Little League game?

If you own a dry cleaner, can you post a sign in the window offering free suit cleaning to someone unemployed and down on their luck who has a job interview?

If you're the owner of any business that has employees, can you occasionally focus on them? The occasional free lunch? Gift certificate for their birthday? Something that says "We value you and what you do."

Shannon Maida will *only* stay at the Bryant Park Hotel when she visits New York, because the staff takes an extra minute to play with her daughter and let her pretend that she's the Eloise of Bryant Park. Shannon estimates that she's turned over ten people into Zombie Loyalists for that hotel. That's some serious revenue just for calling a six-year-old "Eloise."

In early 2013, I was on the road in Dubai and was staying at a Ritz-Carlton. By now we all know about the Ritz's hospitality. But the hotel did something that cost it probably 48 cents and is easily repeatable by anyone in any company.

Upon returning to my room after a ridiculously long day of meetings in the desert, I noticed a note on my bathroom counter, along with a brand-new tube of toothpaste. Turns out I was running out. I was clueless to this, as I am to most things.

Of course, I was floored. And of course, the first thing I did was take a photo of it, and, of course, I pushed that photo out to my social networks.

My social networks blew up, and the brand awareness of the amazing service at Ritz-Carlton shot up a little bit as well. I personally know two people who made reservations at this specific hotel when they traveled to Dubai in the following months, and they both said this picture was what pushed them over the edge to do it.

Cost to the hotel? Probably about 48 cents. Result? Well, let's just say reservations at the Ritz-Carlton Dubai aren't cheap. How's that for some customer service ROI?

Bring random amazement into normal situations.

What can you do to make this happen?

A few years ago, a family with an autistic daughter went to a local Chili's for lunch. The daughter, who loves cheeseburgers, was distraught to find hers "broken"—that is, cut down the middle.

Her father asked politely if his child could get a new "unbroken" cheeseburger, to which the waitress responded directly to the child, apologizing for bringing her a broken cheeseburger. Even the manager got into the act, apologizing and bringing out an "unbroken" one for her to eat.

The child was thrilled, of course, and the story, including a photo of the child kissing the cheeseburger, went viral, being featured on *The Today Show,* and tons and tons of websites. What great exposure for Chili's, which probably resulted in more business, but equally important, made it a great breeding ground for Zombie Loyalist parents everywhere.

In my work with customers around the world to help them build Zombie Loyalists, two things have consistently proven to be true:

1. On a whole, companies are tremendously afraid of trying new things.
2. Rarely do customers expect the world. Far more often, they don't expect much at all.

Regarding point one, you'll find that more often than not, employees are afraid of getting in trouble for not doing things by the book. Management is afraid of rocking the boat, and the CEO isn't aware that there are problems. It's a repetitive cycle that's only broken when something hugely negative happens and the company needs to reinvent itself (Domino's) or when a new CEO comes into town and has a singular goal of shaking things up (Netflix).

The solution to that, I've found, is to get companies into the mind-set of understanding that if you do things the way they've always been done, you'll get the same results you've always been getting. Once you try new things, the world opens up to you.

As for point two, being able to do those little things will keep you recalled. Doing them without an agenda, when the customer isn't even thinking of you, will get you remembered. There's a huge difference between "recalling" something and actually "remembering" it. You *recall* having dinner last week. You *remember* how someone at the restaurant where you had that amazing meal took time out of their day to call and invite you back since they hadn't seen you in a while.

What can you do to remind customers that you're there for them, even when they haven't been there for you in a while?

AMERICAN EXPRESS

American Express is one of those companies that knows me. It should. I've been using Amex for close to 20 years, and I try to put as much of my life on the card as I can.

What I love most about Amex is that it doesn't bother me. When the company does something, it's almost always a benefit to me. It never tries to upsell me. It never calls me randomly and tries to get me to sign up for a more expensive card. If the company reaches out, it's because it is doing something for my benefit. A few points about the relationship Amex has with its customers:

It's about Taking the Time to Get to Know Each Customer

Amex knows me. The customer file Amex has on me must be several gigabytes at least, and I'm totally, 100 percent okay with that. As I said above, in all the time I've had an Amex, it's *never* tried to upsell me, it's never spammed me, it's never done anything insidious with my information. As such, I trust the company, and I'm happy to tell it anything it wants to know. Why? Because I know the information it collects on me helps it make my life easier.

An example: Last year I received a replacement card, despite still having my regular card in my possession. When I called to ask why it was sent to me, I was told the following:

> Mr. Shankman, we notice that you take multiple overseas trips per year. If you look at your new card, you'll notice a little PIN chip embedded in it. In virtually every country but the United States, the PIN chip method is the preferred, and much safer way of paying for a transaction. We also noticed that the last time you were overseas, you were unable to use your card at an automated Metro station, because your card lacked a PIN

chip. We noticed this with several of our customers who travel overseas, so we're implementing a PIN chip system for those customers. Since you're one of them, we hope this will make your international travel a little easier.

There was no charge, and Amex didn't even ask me if I wanted it. No forms or paperwork. *Amex simply saw an opportunity to make my life easier and took it.* End result? I got off a plane in Stockholm last month, exhausted from a red-eye flight, and walked over to the subway station. Instead of having to wait in a line 25 deep for the one customer rep there, I slid my PIN-enabled card into the credit card slot and had a round-trip ticket in my hands in five seconds. That's ease of use. That's customer service. I can tell you that I couldn't do that with any other card I carry.

YOUR IMPLEMENTATION: What do you know about your customers that you can use to their benefit in a noncreepy way? Do some of your customers buy the same thing each month like clockwork? Offer monthly reshipping, charged to the same credit card, and frame it as "making their lives easier." An online bike store I use all the time does this in another way—I usually go through two to three pairs of gloves a season, because I tend to fall down a lot. Stupid clips. Anyhow, on my last order, I didn't order any gloves, and the company sent me a pair anyway, with a little note attached—"Figured you might be close to needing a new pair." Stellar. Just stellar. Think I'll ever use another bike store online? Heck no. And do I tell everyone about this one? I do indeed. *Learn to notice when you have an opportunity to make a customer's life easier, and do it. Don't ask. Just do it. Or, to put it another way: Bring random amazement into normal situations.*

It's about Perfectly Walking the Fine Line between "Protective" and "Creepy"

For this section of the book, I went in and broke down my last month's Amex bill by type of charge: 49 web charges, 37 in-person charges, and 22 monthly repeat charges. I looked at a few months prior, and they were all pretty much the same. Most people are big fans of patterns. While I might travel all over the world, my flights and hotels are booked the exact same way by my assistant, and diapers and cat food are monthly repeat orders. No doubt that before I know it, "diapers" will be replaced by "teenager food," but that's neither here nor there. The point is, Amex knows my patterns (and, by default, my assistant's patterns). It also knows all the weird stuff I'm into, and it understands that it's not out of the ordinary to see an expensive client dinner one night and a charge from Joe's Skydiving Shack the next morning. I love that—my life isn't interrupted by Amex checking things on a regular basis, but I know I'm protected when it's needed. As such, when my assistant's card (which is a subcard of my account) started showing random charges at KFC, Popeye's Chicken, and Home Depot (i.e., places Meagan or I would rarely, if ever, go), Amex flagged it, contacted me, and, sure enough, we'd been defrauded.

Granted, American Express spends millions each year to prevent credit card fraud, as it should. But even the way it handled the problem was amazing. Someone from Amex called me, and within ten minutes, the card was canceled and a new card was FedExed to me, we'd gone down my assistant's entire list of charges for the month and removed all that weren't hers, and, most important, Amex followed up twice more that month to check in. Meagan didn't have to take any time out of her life at all. And as I've said multiple times, time is by far the most valuable resource for most folks these days.

YOUR IMPLEMENTATION: Customers are going to have problems. Things are going to happen, and customers are going to need your help in fixing them. It could be something as simple as a broken purchase or as complex as a screwup on a million-dollar order. How you respond, how you make customers feel better, determines the amount of love they're going to have for you. And remember, lovers and haters both talk. They tell others, good or bad.

It's about Having Options

I haven't had a physical bill from Amex in perhaps 12 years. It's all done online, and I can choose when. I can pay from my computer, from my phone, whatever. This isn't exclusive to Amex, obviously, but I can tell you that in 12 years, the system has never failed me. Yet my accountant, whom I value tremendously, requires a physical check every three months. As if I'm even home every three months. Needless to say, his payment is often late. Not intentionally, mind you, but often. If I could auto-debit his bill from my checking account, he'd get paid on time, every time.

YOUR IMPLEMENTATION: What can do you to make your clients' or customers' lives easier when it comes to you getting paid, and in the process, get paid faster and more reliably? Can you implement Square? Can you discount 10 percent for immediate payment? Can you set up a better online solution? I've done tests with how I bill—I almost *always* get paid faster when the client can do it electronically. Besides, who really uses physical checks anymore, anyway? Going to the bank? Ain't nobody got time for that!

It's about Your Customers and Clients Knowing Help Is There When They Need It

On a trip to Colombia a few years ago for a speaking gig, I made an incorrect car reservation, and the driver who was supposed to pick me up thought it was the next day. Colombia isn't necessarily the type of place where you just want to jump in the first available cab from the airport. It was 1 a.m. New York time, and my car service place in New York that booked the reservation wasn't answering. In desperation, I called Amex, and within ten minutes, a concierge had a car on its way to me. Nothing else mattered at that point; I was getting a trusted vehicle to take me to my hotel. Problem solved. The level of trust I have in Amex is usually reserved only for family members and my assistant. That's huge.

ADDENDUM TO THE ABOVE: A while back, my grandma was in the hospital, and I was away on business. I had no clue as to what to get her, but I wanted to get her something. I wasn't up on the latest gifts for people over 90 in hospitals, so on a whim, I called Amex. I just told the person I spoke with to choose. Within three hours, a five-foot-high plush kangaroo was sitting at my grandma's bedside. She named it "Hoppy." She invited everyone on the floor to visit Hoppy. She was released from the hospital two days later. My father, to this day, believes she got better because Hoppy made my grandma the center of attention. Ha. While that may or may not be true, this much is: Amex came through for me and my 90-something-year-old grandma. That's simply ace. My grandmother has since passed on, but Hoppy lives in the very hospital in which she was treated, making patients happy every day.

YOUR IMPLEMENTATION: How can you go out of your way when it's called for to do something unexpected? Do your employees feel empowered to do this on their own? If not, can you give them that empowerment? If you can't, what can you change to make sure you can? I can't stress how important it is to not only give your employees that empowerment, but even more, to make sure they always feel free to use it. Empowered employees solve problems. When customers have their problems solved, they become Zombie Loyalists, and they bring you new customers, and so on, and so on.

Bring random amazement into normal situations.

It's about Offering That Trust Back to Your Customer

Let's clear something up. Amex is famous for "no credit limit." From the research I've done, that's not exactly what it means. It's famous for no *preset* credit limit, which is a huge difference. Essentially, it means that as long as you pay your due balance by when it's due and aren't late, the chances of you going "over" your limit are limited, and if you ever are dinged with a "not enough credit," and you have a good history with Amex, you can call and it'll usually be taken care of. Now, I obviously don't work for Amex, nor do I have any inside info, but this is what I've heard.

How does that apply to me? Well, I've had trips come up at the last minute—a speaking gig where the keynote got sick (or even arrested—I'm serious). Could I be in Europe, or Asia, or wherever, in two days? There's a level of confidence that comes with knowing that I can say yes, make the sale, close the deal, give the speech, in person, because Amex will back me up and let the ridiculously priced walk-up airline fare go through. It's mutual trust. That's hugely important to me.

YOUR IMPLEMENTATION: Can you be more trusting of your customers who have a good track record with you? Can you be flexible on their payment terms? Can you give your customers the knowledge that if they need you to help take their business (or just their lives) to the next level, you can be counted on to do that? That's how you convert loyal customers into Zombie Loyalists, customers for life and beyond.

My dad has an Amex card, I have one, and you know my daughter will have one. Why? The brand continues to prove itself over and over again. I wish nothing but the same for your company.

So let's close this chapter with a quick review:

- Reach out to your customers and say hi with something of value to them *without selling to them*.
- Give them something that they can't get anywhere else—an experience that only they can have, and yes, can brag about if they so desire. (And chances are, they will desire.)
- Check in on them, not in a creepy/stalky way, but in a way that makes them recognize that you understand how important they are to you.
- Be *top of mind*. It worked for Barry Diller.
- Empower your employees to do this. Every single one of them!

And finally . . .

- *Bring random amazement into normal situations.*

By the way . . . Why do I keep saying that? Two reasons.

1. It's true. Bringing random amazement into normal situations will keep your customers and clients loving you, coming back for more, talking about you, and staying Zombie Loyalists to your business who in turn go out and infect their friends for you.
2. The second reason I keep saying that? Well, I like to make things easy to remember. This is a book about zombies, right? I mean, it's a book about customer service, but set around a theme of zombies.

Okay. So . . . what do Zombies eat? *Zombies eat brains.*

Bring
Random
Amazement
Into
Normal
Situations

Bring Random Amazement into Normal Situations, or BRAINS.
Zombies eat brains. Feed your zombies BRAINS, and they'll stay loyal to your business for this life, and long after they become undead.
Go have fun.

10

EVENTUAL ZOMBIE SOCIETAL TAKEOVER AND BEYOND

HOW TO KEEP THE LOYALTY GOING AND BUILD THE NEXT GENERATION OF ZOMBIE LOYALISTS

Remember; no matter how desperate the situation seems, time spent thinking clearly is never time wasted.

—Max Brooks, *The Zombie Survival Guide*

As a wrap-up, here's how to make sure your Zombie Loyalists continue to build your business for you, for generations to come. (Alternate ending: How to enjoy what happens when the Zombies eat your brains.)

Awhile back, I was taking an Uber car from a meeting in San Francisco to the airport. As I mentioned earlier, Uber works on the basis of reviews, with the higher-reviewed drivers getting better chances at better jobs.

Upon entering the car, I noticed two power cords hanging from the driver's seat, one for Apple products and one for Android. I asked the driver if I could use them.

"That's why they're here, sir," he said.

"Does Uber provide them to all their drivers?" I asked.

"No, sir. I decided that since most of my passengers were business travelers, it would be a benefit to them to have both chargers, so I bought them and bought an adapter to plug them into my car."

Arriving at the airport with a bit more juice than when I left, I obviously gave my driver five stars. If you figure that each charger cost $10 and one adapter costs $15, then my driver spent $35 one time, to repeatedly make customers happy.

I looked my driver up after I reviewed him. He had a 4.9 rating, pretty much the highest rating you can get on Uber. I've never seen a 5.0.

I don't know the math here, but for kicks, let's say our driver gets ten jobs a day at 4.9 stars, as opposed to eight jobs a day for someone who had 4.5 stars. That one-time $35 investment paid for itself in less than a morning, and the revenue he gets from his ratings will continue to grow for him.

And they say there's no money in being nice.

Welcome to the future, where the sharing economy will be everywhere, and the concept of the trusted peer review will determine who shops where, how much they spend, whether they come back, and if they bring friends.

In other words, the future economy will run on the trusted network, and entry into the trusted network will be achieved by relevance to the customer. Let me explain.

Today, sites like Yelp and Trip Advisor are the basis for how people find out what other people think about almost anything—hotels, restaurants, airlines, you name it. If someone's used it, there's a review about it somewhere. And for several years, that's been an acceptable way of thinking.

But that's starting to go away. Not only did Yelp have thousands of consumer complaints in the past few years about questionable business practices, but the bigger picture (and one that will affect all "anonymous review" sites) is this:

Why the heck are you basing choices about where you stay, what you eat, what you visit, or what airline you fly on reviews from people you've never even met, have no basis for trusting, and, for all you know, could be working at or against the company in question? Think about that for a second.

In the very near future, you won't have to.

As we're seeing more and more every day, every interaction we have, whether with a company, a friend, a service provider, or anyone else, will be done within our network. How that interaction plays out will determine the relevance of that person, company, friend, or service provider within our network.

Imagine, if you will, a giant lava lamp. Lava lamps were everywhere years ago. Oil mixed with water, and a lamp at the bottom that heated up the oil, which would float to the top. When it cooled, it would come back down and get heated again, thus floating back to the top, making pretty colors in the water. Repeat, repeat, repeat. Trippy, man.

The hotter the oil, the higher it rose in the lamp. The cooler it was, the quicker it descended.

Now imagine the water in that lava lamp is your network. It's everything in your life, all encapsulated in the digital equivalent of a globe. Everywhere you go, it's with you, you can access it from anywhere, and it is amazingly good at figuring out where you are, what time it is, where you might be going, what you might be hungry for, what you might feel like doing, or with whom you might want to chat.

The millions of drops of oil floating all around that water? Well, that's every person, business, and service that you've ever interacted with in any capacity at all. One of those drops of oil represents the guy who towed your car when you got stuck on vacation outside Phoenix ten years ago. Another drop? That represents your mom. Yet another drop? The coffee shop you visited once on a business trip to Miami. Yet another drop? The guy you exchanged business cards with at a bar in Tokyo when you were 32. Yet another drop? Your daughter's third-grade teacher.

But still more drops. One from the McDonald's on 23rd and Pine. Another is the hotel you stayed in that had that water leak in the bathroom that no employee cared enough to fix, despite the numerous times you called. Yet another drop? The car dealership from which you've bought your last four Infiniti coupes, and another is your wife or husband. Yet another is the wine shop where you bought that bottle of Scotch for the man who introduced you to your biggest client. Another is that man, and another is your biggest client. A few more? Your second-grade teacher, the girl you dated four times in college, and your mail carrier.

Okay. So . . . what's the light at the bottom acting as the heat source? Brace yourselves for this one, although, if you've been reading the whole way through, I bet you'll already know . . .

Relevance.

Relevance is going to power the world. It's going to be relevance that determines what you see in your Facebook feed. It's going to be relevance that tells you what restaurants are near you. Relevance will connect you with a piano teacher for your 11-year-old son and a housekeeper for your new condo. Relevance will find you the right dentist and the best cruise ship that only sails in the winter.

Relevance is going to determine where you buy a house and who you use as your Realtor. It's going to pick the vet who saves your dog's life and will tell you where you'll hold your twentieth-anniversary dinner.

Relevance is going to be the energy source that powers the new consumer and business economies, the force that drives all commerce, and the inertia that keeps the universe outwardly expanding.

Relevance will bring revenue to your business and line customers up around the block for your latest creation. Relevance will determine which companies win, which companies lose, and which companies own the next 100 years.

Relevance is going to save us, but only if we know what to do. Relevance is going to bring your business to new heights, but only if you know how to channel it. Relevance is going to be more powerful than advertising, more powerful than public relations, more powerful than advertising, and more powerful than Superman.

Relevance is going to change the world, and in a lot of cases in this book and in your everyday lives, it already is.

So how will it happen?

Customer service.

Let's face it. In less than five years, every company will be online in all the same places. Every company will be advertising in all the same places, and every company will be competing for the same customers.

There will be minimal difference between what pizza place A or pizza place B can offer you in terms or price or quality. The same goes for car dealer 1 and car dealer 2.

What will differentiate? Customer service.

How each customer leaves after an interaction will determine the fate of the company with which he or she interacted.

Everything you do, everything you love, everything you hate, everything with which you interact will be on the network. Your enjoyment or dislike of that interaction will determine where on your network it ranks. This will go from personal to commercial to business and back again. The gamut will be run via your network.

Sound crazy? It's not. Sound Orwellian? Not really. . . . It's already happening, and we're actually better off for it. But what's going to change is the level of personal connection with which it happens.

Let's explore.

It's four years from now, and Mark is sitting at a bar in a hotel lobby with a few minutes to kill before he has to leave for dinner. The restaurant where he'll be eating with his work colleagues is close to the hotel, and a few days ago, back in the office, when he pulled up Google Maps and searched for "Restaurants near Sheraton Downtown Los Angeles," several came up, but the first one in the list had a star next to it, along with the Facebook profile photo of his close friend Michael, as well as a status update from a few months earlier, where Michael had raved about the New York strip steak he'd had there. This told Mark that Michael had been to this specific restaurant before and had liked it, so he made a reservation through Open Table, which was connected to Google Maps.

As Mark works on his drink at the bar, checking his email, he strikes up a conversation with Laura, an attractive woman next to him. Turns out they're both in Los Angeles from New York City and both are here on business.

Mark and his new friend share a drink, but then Mark has to leave for dinner. He texts his new friend his phone number, so now they each have the other's number. The number of the other is automatically added to each of their address books, both on their phones and in the cloud, and because they've set their privacy settings to allow anyone who has their number to also know their email address automatically, the network adds the email address of each into their address book as well.

Two days later, Mark is headed back to New York, and he texts his new friend Laura, asking when she'll be leaving for the city. She texts back that she's on a red-eye flight tomorrow. He suggests that they try to grab another drink Friday night in New York. She agrees.

At this point, Mark and Laura have interacted in two separate text discussions, or, to put it another way, their network has been made aware of a new connection: two text discussions and an in-person connection at the bar in the hotel. Three separate touch points.

Back in New York, Mark texts Laura the name of a bar and a time to meet. When Laura texts back "great, see you there," the network notes the sentiment of the text as positive and, based on that, automatically adds a calendar entry into Laura's calendar on her phone, Mark at [name of bar], for 7 p.m. on Friday. It also links to the text in her phone, in case she forgets who she's meeting.

Those were touch points 4 through 6.

When Mark and Laura both arrive at the bar, the network notes their close proximity, (the same way it did when they first texted in LA) in combination with both calendar appointments. Touch points 7 and 8.

Drinks go well, so Mark asks Laura to dinner. She agrees for the following week, so Mark heads to OpenTable and makes a reservation, putting her email in so OpenTable will send her the table invite. The restaurant he chose was one picked by Michael for a first date with his now girlfriend, two years ago. It comes highly recommended.

When they both show up at dinner, that's touch point 10. At touch point 10, the network simply says "Okay, you're friends."

All of a sudden, Mark and Laura are friends online, and they're sharing with each other whatever they've allowed the network to share to friends with 10 to 99 touch points.

There's no "friend requests" anymore. There's no "Find me on Facebook or Google Plus." There's simply *life*.

Fast forward about six months, and Mark and Laura are boyfriend and girlfriend. They spend a ton of time together and, at least once a month, go back to the restaurant where they had their first date.

When Mark signs onto his network in the morning (doesn't matter which network, it could be Facebook, or Google, or whatever, they'll all be connected), Laura's updates are the first thing he sees. When Laura signs on to hers, Mark's updates are the first thing she sees.

They're both top of mind in each other's worlds. Online, both of their droplets of oil are the top drops in each other's social lava lamps.

The places they go, the restaurants they visit, the theaters they attend, all of them will be high in both of their networks, as long as they keep visiting them. They won't have to "like" the page of a restaurant or leave a positive review somewhere. The interaction, the sentiment they show when talking about their experience: that will determine their review automatically. They like the place? That'll show up. They didn't enjoy it? That will too.

They stop going to a place they normally went to? Well, that place won't show up in their stream anywhere near as much anymore, until eventually they don't see it at all, and it won't be "recommended" by Mark or Laura when their friends look up a place to go.

See where we're going here? It's all about relevance. If that first-date restaurant wants to stay in Mark and Laura's stream and, as such, continue to be top of mind and get their business, and the business of all of their friends and acquaintances, then *the restaurant must provide an amazing experience to them, every single time they go there.*

If the restaurant does that, Mark and Laura's circle will continue to be influenced to eat there by Mark and Laura, *automatically.* But the second that restaurant screws up, it's lights out in their feed, and by default, that restaurant says good-bye to Mark and Laura's automatic recommendation to all their friends.

It's going to come down to customer service and mindshare.

As a company treats you well, the *sentiment of your interaction* will determine the relevance of that business in your stream within your network. The same goes for every other business in everyone else's network. The most interesting part? Customers won't have to "share" their experience by writing a review or posting that they liked or didn't like a business. The sentiment of everything they do— an Instagram photo of a meal, a Tweet about waiting in line too long, even the frequency of their visits to that business, they will all determine that customer's happiness or displeasure with that business—automatically. And that's why customer service will continue to matter more and more.

As I said earlier, why should I rely on Yelp or Trip Advisor, or another site with reviews from people I don't know, if I can simply log on to Google Maps, and it'll show me where my friends have eaten, stayed, vacationed, bought from, flown, played, and been entertained, or as I go to a travel site to look up flights, I get a little note in the window that says "your friend Ty flew this route two months ago on Virgin Airlines, and it seems that he had a great trip. Would you like to see fares on Virgin for this route?"

Now here's the kicker: Let's say Mark and Laura (remember them? From the hotel bar in LA?) want to go to Fiji, but none of their friends has ever been. How will they get their trusted information if no one in their network can provide it?

Easy. The network knows who Mark and Laura's friends are *as well as their friends' friends*. So if Laura doesn't know anyone who's been to Fiji, but Laura's friend Allison knows Jennifer, and Jennifer lived in Fiji for a year, then Laura will see Jennifer's recommendations. Why is that still trustworthy? Because on the random off chance that Jennifer gives bogus information to Laura, that reflects badly on Allison. And Allison wouldn't let that happen.

See where we're going? The future will be a network of trusted relationships and trusted recommendations.

The thing is, this is already happening. Ever log in to Facebook when you're traveling and see updates from people you haven't thought about in forever? That's geographical targeting. The network knows you're somewhere new and is showing you things relevant to you in that location.

The concept of checking in to locations will disappear as well—it'll be automatic, unless you don't want it to be. (That's another important point for those worried that the future won't have any privacy: Quite the opposite—shut off your phone, and your privacy will be almost guaranteed—much more than it is now.)

What does this mean for your business?

It means advertising, marketing, and public relations will take a backseat to *personal recommendation*. Nothing will be stronger than the personal recommendation; it will be even more powerful than it already is now.

A billboard might interest me, an ad on a website might catch my attention for a second, but an "Oh, my assistant Meagan shopped there, and look, she loved what she bought, and she's one of the most stylish people I know, so I should go there too" will be the strongest call to action in the world.

Want to survive? Know your customers. Know them before they walk in the door. Eleven Madison Park, a Michelin Three-Star restaurant, now makes Googling and Facebooking guests before they arrive a standard practice.

The website *Ars Technica,* following a story from *Grub Street,* reported:

> The maitre d' in question, Justin Roller, says he tries to ascertain things like whether a couple is coming to the restaurant for an anniversary, and if so, which anniversary that is. If it's a birthday, for instance, he wants to wish them "Happy Birthday" when they arrive. He'll scan for photos of the guests in chef's whites or posed with wine glasses, which suggest they might be chefs or sommeliers themselves.
>
> It goes deeper: If a particular guest appears to hail from Montana, Roller will try to pair up the table with a server who is from Montana. "Same goes for guests who own jazz clubs, who can be paired with a sommelier that happens to be into jazz," writes Grub Street.[1]

Does that sound a bit creepy to you? If it does, remember this: In 1998, virtually no one shopped online. Why? "It was too dangerous. Hackers could steal my credit card information!" Remember those days?

The future is coming. The best advice I can offer to help you let your business master it is simple: You can't fake customer service, you can't half ass it. It needs to be a culture from the chief executive all the way down to the lowest employee on the totem pole. It needs to incorporate human resources and how it selects employees for hire; the employees need to want to make things better than they are.

It's not a call to never make mistakes. That's impossible. But it *is a call to make sure that when they're made, they're corrected.* It's a call to teach everyone in your business that if a customer leaves in any way but thrilled, the business has failed. Because in the long run, if that happens a lot, the business *will* fail, and no amount of brand awareness can save you.

Bring random amazement into normal situations (BRAINS) every day to breed Zombie Loyalist armies for your business. Focus on doing the basics brilliantly, and the rest will follow. You don't have to deliver a steak to the airport if a smile and "Happy birthday, Mr. Evans!" will accomplish the same.

Go for the occasional home run. Show up randomly with doughnuts; why not? Try for the impossible whenever you can. But focus on creating the amazing every day. Call customers who haven't been in for a while and check in on them. Don't sell. Check in.

Spend every day making sure that when each customer leaves, signs off, clicks "purchase," or pays the bill, that customer is smiling. If they're not, don't let them out the door until they are.

BRING RANDOM AMAZEMENT INTO
NORMAL SITUATIONS (BRAINS)

Do it every day, and your Zombie Loyalists will line up to buy from you, they'll march across the earth with your logo on their flag, they'll beat down anyone who tries to disparage you. They'll make you famous for all the right reasons.

Go forth and provide amazement. Have fun doing it. Make sure your employees have fun doing it. Zombie Loyalists breed well only in the presence of happy employees who like to have fun.

Go be brilliant. Raise the bar of what we expect customer service to be in this world.

As I've said in many chapters already, I want to hear from you. Love the book? Get some ideas out of it? Want some help implementing? I want to know!

I'll even do you one better—I travel all over the world talking about this stuff. If I'm ever in your city, reach out to me and I'll buy you a cup of coffee, and we can brainstorm some strategies to breed you some Zombies, okay?

My email is peter@shankman.com, my Twitter handle is @peter shankman, and on Facebook, I'm http://facebook.com/petershank man. LinkedIn is www.linkedin.com/in/petershankman/, and Google Plus is https://plus.google.com/+PeterShankmanOfficial. I'd love to hear from you.

Go. Create Zombie Loyalists. Your army is ready to fight for you.

Thanks for reading.

NOTES

CHAPTER 2: IDENTIFYING THE BARRIERS TO ZOMBIE LOYALTY

1. "2012 Global Consumer Pulse Research Key Findings," Accenture, http://www.accenture.com/SiteCollectionDocuments/PDF/Accenture-Global-Consumer-Pulse-Research-Study-2012-Key-Findings.pdf.
2. *Harvard Business Review on Increasing Customer Loyalty* (Boston, MA: Harvard Business Press Books, 2011), http://hbr.org/product/harvard-business-review-on-increasing-customer-loy/an/10322-PDF-ENG.
3. "2012 Global Customer Service Barometer: Findings, in the United States," research report prepared for American Express, http://about.americanexpress.com/news/docs/2012x/axp_2012gcsb_us.pdf.

CHAPTER 3: LEADING YOUR COMPANY TO AN OPTIMAL LEVEL OF BREEDING READINESS TO CREATE ZOMBIE LOYALISTS

1. Mark Hrywna, Patrick Sullivan, and Martin C. Daks, "NPT's Best Nonprofits to Work For 2014," *The Nonprofit Times*, April 1, 2014, http://www.thenonprofittimes.com/wp-content/uploads/2014/04/BestNonprofits-2014.pdf.

CHAPTER 4: NOW THAT YOU'RE READY TO BREED, LET'S INFECT YOUR FIRST CUSTOMER

1. www.skratchlabs.com.

CHAPTER 6: SPREADING THE WORD

1. Kashmir Hill, "How Target Figured Out a Teen Girl Was Pregnant Before Her Father Did," *Forbes*, February 16, 2012, http://www.forbes.com/sites/kashmirhill/2012/02/16/how-target-figured-out-a-teen-girl-was-pregnant-before-her-father-did/.
2. Chris Morran, "This Is the Kind of Message Restaurant Employees Should Be Leaving on Receipts," *Consumerist*, January 7, 2013. http://consumerist.com/2013/01/07/this-is-the-kind-of-message-restaurant-employees-should-be-leaving-on-receipts/.

3. Chris Morran, "Some Thoughts from Red Robin Manager Who Gave Free Meal to Pregnant Customer," *Consumerist*, January 9, 2013, http://consumerist.com/2013/01/09/some-thoughts-from-red-robin-manager-who-gave-free-meal-to-pregnant-customer/.

4. *Mad Men,* season no. 1, episode no. 1, "Smoke Gets in Your Eyes," directed by Alan Taylor, written by Matthew Weiner, AMC, July 19, 2007.

CHAPTER 7: YOU LOST A ZOMBIE!

1. Nichole Kelly, "One Bad Experience Can Ruin a Lifetime of Loyalty," *Social Media Explorer,* August 13, 2013, http://www.socialmediaexplorer.com/digital-marketing/one-bad-experience-can-ruin-a-lifetime-of-loyalty/.

CHAPTER 8: YOU FORGOT TO FEED YOUR ZOMBIES!

1. Adrian Campos, "Why Domino's Spent Millions to Fix It's Pizza," *The Motley Fool*, November 20, 2013, http://www.fool.com/investing/general/2013/11/20/why-dominos-spent-millions-to-fix-its-pizza.aspx.

2. Carmel Lobello, "How Netflix Came Back from the Dead and Beat HBO," *TheStreet*, April 23, 2013, http://theweek.com/article/index/243139/how-netflix-came-back-from-the-dead-and-beat-hbo.

3. Ibid.

4. Antoine Gara, "T-Mobile's Epic Market Share Grab," *TheStreet*, February 26, 2014, http://www.thestreet.com/story/12457873/1/t-mobiles-epic-market-share-grab.html.

CHAPTER 10: EVENTUAL ZOMBIE SOCIETAL TAKEOVER AND BEYOND

1. Casey Johnston, "When the Restaurant You Googled Googles You Back," *Ars Technica,* April 13, 2014, http://arstechnica.com/staff/2014/04/when-the-restaurant-you-googled-googles-you-back/.

INDEX